*The longest part of the journey is said to be
the passing of the gate.*

—MARCUS TERENTIUS VARRO

Believe . . . there's a change for you and me.

—DAMIEN RICE

CONTENTS

Disclaimer

The meditations, exercises, and personal experiences of the author, his students, and clients included in this book are for interest purposes only.

The exercises presented have been tested in many workshops, client healings, and other real-life applications. No harm has ever come to any participant as a result. It *is important*, however, to act sensibly and responsibly when undertaking any introspective or spiritually challenging work. Your attention is especially drawn to the author's experiences with the elements—firewalking, breathing under water, the "leap of faith," and the "burial of the warrior"—and you are advised *not* to attempt these yourself without expert supervision from someone familiar with and able to teach you these techniques.

Any application of the approaches in this book remains at the reader's own risk and the authors and publishers disclaim any liability arising directly or indirectly from their use.

The Four Gates to Freedom

Do you really want to be free and happy—or are you addicted to your sorrow? A lot of people *are* addicted and they either don't know it or don't know what to do about it. Herein lies the problem: programmed by society to believe that happiness, love, and freedom can only be acquired through power, possessions, and people, men and women have lost the one thing that really matters: *themselves*. Many, sadly, will never learn the truth of who they are, of "who it is that lives," beyond the labels given them by the world.

You are not one of these people.

You have been drawn to this book because life has chosen this moment to reveal something of itself to you through the writings of Ross Heaven, its author. You are right on time to read what you are about to read.

The incongruence and tension that results from living a life according to who we *think* we are, and not the truth of who we *really* are, is at the heart of our pain and unhappiness. This suffering, which we could also call ignorance of truth, is what you and I, knowingly or unknowingly, desire to be free of. Beyond this ignorance lies the truth, the thing we most need and desire to be reunited with.

This truth—intelligence, consciousness, soul, or spirit—is the goodness, the life, the love, the happiness and peace that we were and wish to be once more.

And there is life's great paradox. Billions of men and women are searching for the truth outside of themselves and not within. As a person with amnesia might walk out of his house in an attempt to find his house, so we walk out of our truth looking for our truth. This continues until the day of awakening, the day that we start to see the world *as it is* and not as we *think* it is. This marks the first sign of our impending freedom.

So . . . are you courageous? Are you willing to let go of the past and face the shadows? Are you ready to descend deep—beyond the mind—into the stillness, the Void from which you arose? A *yes* or even a *maybe* is sufficient. You are ready to be free and to meet your guide, Ross Heaven. He will escort you through the Four Gates to Freedom.

Ross has drawn upon his considerable personal experience to create an extraordinary book, one which, I believe, details many of the necessary insights and practical tools that, when lived with our total and conscious participation, will enable us to start living our lives as *we choose* to live them. All that is required is our commitment and willingness to become all that we are.

I wish you every success.

DR. MARK ATKINSON,
MBBS, BSc (HONS), FRIPHH, FCMA, BETD, SAC DIP

Dr. Mark Atkinson is the founder of the Whole Body Healing Clinic in London and a pioneer in the fields of holistic medicine, healing, and personal transformation. He is an author and the complementary health expert for *Now* magazine and *Good Morning Television* in the United Kingdom.

PREFACE

IN THE BEGINNING . . .

Legends tell that Mima O was an old man when he arrived on the shores of Japan in 600 B.C.E. His travels, from his homeland of Babylon, had been long and full of adventure. In India he had been revered as a Brahman, and he had gathered many other titles of respect—wise man, holy man, seer, sage—in the lands along his way. It is said that he carried a rosary of seventy-two magical beads, which he used to see the future, and that he was learned in astronomy, astrology, philosophy, medicine, and what would come to be known as psychology, as well as in the warrior arts.

Babylon was one of the most advanced cultures of its time, rivaling Egypt; its people were explorers and seekers of wisdom. There are some, in fact, who believe that the wise men who would later visit Jesus began their journey in Babylon, and that the Magi were members of a secret and ancient society (to which Mima O may also have belonged) with its own rituals, observances, and teachings.

Mima O had traveled enough when he reached Japan, though, so he settled there and began his great life's work: the crafting of the *Amatsu Tatara* ("Heaven's Place"),* a document that was to achieve sacred status as a work of hidden and holy truths. The *Amatsu Tatara* contained

---

*I am grateful to sensei Gary Arthur for his instruction in the *Amatsu Tatara* and his training in some of its practical applications. Gary is the UK Faculty for the Stephen Hayes training method and has a website at www.toshindo.co.uk.

information that only a great master of the arcane arts could know, including methods for communicating with God, sensing the future and altering its course, physical skills such as movement and breathing for health, and mental arts for skillful thinking and the knowledge of truth.

Few people were to see this document, but those who did were changed by it. They say it held answers to life's enduring questions and had a power of its own. It was not a document that promised its readers fame and wealth or godlike abilities, however; its intention was far more significant and radical than that. It revealed how all people, regardless of status, gender, background, beliefs, or perceived abilities could achieve their two most essential desires, the search for which has always motivated us: *freedom* and *happiness*.

The promise of the *Amatsu Tatara* was that you can have *anything* you want—*including* fame, wealth, and godlike abilities if these are what truly make you happy and free. And you can have them all through the exercise of a power that is already within you and simply needs to be "remembered"—discovered and released.

Before Mima O died, he bequeathed the *Amatsu Tatara* to the safekeeping of the Nakatomi family, one of the leading schools *(ryu)* of Shinto, the shamanic religion of Japan. Nakatomi Ryu later became Kukishin Ryu and absorbed Taoist, Shugendo, Samurai, and other essentially shamanic, spiritual, and warrior teachings. It is from this school that the wisdom of Mima O was passed down the generations to the Abe, Mononobe, and Otomo families so that history would be preserved, and this knowledge from the land of the Magi could be taught to others. Through these families, the *Amatsu Tatara* became the foundation for the living arts of the Ninja, the mysterious shadow warriors that history would come to regard as almost superhuman in their physical, mental, emotional, and spiritual abilities—so much so, in fact, that they were believed by some to be *tengu*, supernatural entities, half human–half crow mountain demons, gods of nature and healing: the "Masters of the Void."

Legends tell of the Ninja's ability to bend the laws of nature and control the human mind. They "expounded systems of integrated mind-body awareness, based on personal understanding of the order of the universe," according to Stephen Hayes, who is the first American to be accepted as a student of Masaaki Hatsumi, the thirty-fourth grandmaster of the Ninja arts.[1] They pioneered methods of awareness that were later adopted by Japanese *yamabushi* (mountain warrior-priests) and the warrior-ascetics of the wilderness *(sennin* and *gyoja),* who also became part of the "Ninja Way."

These arts of the Ninja have been transmitted across the ages from *sensei* (master teacher) to student in *dojos* (training temples) that draw their first inspiration and wisdom from the great work of Mima O. In this way, thousands of spiritual warriors and seekers after wisdom have heard the message of the *Amatsu Tatara:* you can have *anything* you want.

INTRODUCTION

WHO WERE THE NINJA?

There is no fixed teaching. All I can provide is an appropriate medicine for a particular ailment.

—BRUCE LEE

When asked to describe Jeet Kune Do, the new fighting style he had developed, Bruce Lee said, "Absorb what is useful; disregard everything else. . . . The art of Jeet Kune Do is simply to simplify. It is being oneself; it is reality in its 'isness' . . . freedom in its primary sense, not limited by attachments, confinements, partialization, complexities . . . [it is] a way of life, a movement toward willpower and control . . . enlightened by intuition."[1]

Although Lee was describing his own system, his words can serve as an introduction to the Ninja, a people whose very way of life was based on the fluid absorption of all that was useful in order to develop their unique perspective on the world and the means of acting effectively within it. Like Lee, their insights and approach came from their observations of nature, from testing and thus discovering what worked from the various spiritual, psychological, and warrior traditions they encountered, and from their study of human beings and their reactions to life's circumstances.

Today we have an image of who these Ninja were because they are

1

once again popular in the collective imagination, turning up in block-buster movies such as *Hero, House of Flying Daggers, Crouching Tiger, Elektra*, the *Kill Bill* series, and even *Batman Begins*! But not much is truly known about them, since they chose secrecy and mystery—invisibility—as part of their warrior strategy. One thing is certain, though—that despite what you might have read or seen in a movie, the Ninja were not black-clad assassins; they were, to quote Jack Hoban, "ordinary people who developed certain skills in order to survive in difficult times."[2]* It was these difficult times, in fact, that shaped them and made them what they were.

Jack Hoban is only the third non-Japanese person in the world to attain the level of senior instructor of the Ninja arts. According to him, the Japanese character *nin* can be interpreted in many ways, all of which have to do with perseverance and endurance. And this is a good way to think of these mysterious figures: as men and women who applied advanced skills of living to persevere and endure in a time when wars were the norm, when harsh levels of taxation were common to fund more of these wars, when people were persecuted for their spiritual and ideological beliefs, and there was a firm injunction to follow the system and not question the authority of those in power. Times very much like today, in fact.

The word *Ninjutsu* (the Way of the Ninja) is often translated as "the art of stealth" or "the art of invisibility." The word implies two things: first, the use of stealth to uncover the hidden self so we can discover our inner truth and know what our real purpose is. Second, the skill of remaining true to ourselves but blending so effectively with the prevailing ways of society that we remain almost unseen, leaving no footprints in the sand, while still achieving our purpose.

At the heart of this is self-awareness. The Way of the Ninja is the way of applied psychology and spirituality—that is, applied to the art of effective living. This psychospiritual approach was first mapped out

---

*In fact, the Ninja did not see themselves as "Ninja" at all (a term that actually was not invented until just after World War II), but as Samurai who had been forced to forfeit their lands, or simply as "people of no name and no art"—*Iga No Mono*.

in the *Amatsu Tatara,* but in a rather obscure form. The secret scrolls contain *tenmon* ("Heaven things") and *chimon* ("Earth things"). The latter—such as how to shoot an arrow straight to its target—are the ones the doctrine most obviously demonstrates; but hidden within this is an entire philosophy of "heaven things," like how to ensure the mental stillness necessary for this level of accuracy—or, basically, *how to get what you want.*

It was said that the tenmon could be understood only by a specially trained priest. The harsh living conditions of the Iga and Koga Mountains, however, where the Ninja made their homes, meant that chimon principles were applied every day in order to ensure physical survival. By working with these Earth things, the Ninja naturally absorbed the Heaven things at their core.

As Hoban puts it, "They felt a close connection to the Earth, similar to the Native Americans, and their lifestyle was one lived according to the laws of Nature, not against it. Ninja were very spiritual people, and their beliefs became an integral part of Ninjutsu. . . .

"Another spiritual influence on the Ninja was Mikkyo . . . a method for enhancing personal power. These methods included the use of secret words and symbols to focus their energy and intentions toward specific goals."[3]

Also among the influences on the Ninja were the Shugendo methods of survival and self-discovery. To the Ninja, using these ascetic as well as physically, emotionally, and spiritually challenging methods might mean subjecting themselves willingly to the hardships of the harsh mountain weather and barren landscape, for example, so they could learn how to draw strength from the Earth itself. They would walk through fire, stand in the downpour of freezing waterfalls, or hang over cliffs to overcome their fears and connect to the powers of nature. In essence, they practiced the arts of subduing the ego so they could become one with all-there-is, pushing themselves to extremes of personal discovery in order to find their power and leave behind their psychological self-limitations. "The mind must be emancipated from old habits, prejudices, restrictive thought processes and even ordinary thought itself. . . . Scratch away all the dirt your being has accumulated and reveal reality in its isness, or in its suchness, or in its nakedness," as Bruce Lee wrote of his own system, some twelve hundred years later.[4]

Ninjutsu is still seen as an inherently Japanese tradition but, in fact, that is not the case. As we have seen, the methods employed by the Ninja originated outside of Japan, many of them stemming from the work of Mima O, who himself had mastered several different disciplines of psychology, spiritual awareness, and mental and physical endurance he encountered during his travels around the world. After the fall of the Tang dynasty in China, many more warriors, philosophers, and spiritual experts arrived in Japan to avoid persecution by the new Chinese rulers, and these newcomers took shelter with the Ninja families, who had always felt themselves to be outside of society and shared a sympathy and common cause with the exiles. Many Ninja were themselves displaced Samurai who had been banished by their rulers after defeats in battle or who realized that warrior slavery was not for them. Ironically, they found comfort and a shared way of life with their once-mortal enemies, the free-thinking and revolutionary Ninja. All of these sources and influences were incorporated into what we now know as Ninjutsu. "Absorb what is useful."

If we really want to sum up the art of the Ninja, therefore, we could say that it is simply what works, taken from wherever, and that it relies on two fundamentals: *Know what you want* and *Know how to get it.*

It is this highly sophisticated model of protopsychology that underpinned the Ninja's actions in the world. What it amounted to, first and foremost, was *know yourself.* Find and face your fears so you can find and live your power. Find your own vision for life, and know the reason for your suffering, so you can follow through on your destiny.

This was inner work, initiatory work, and if it meant walking through fire or hanging from a cliff in order to conquer fear and master the self, then so be it. The first requirement of a spiritual warrior was— and is—*Do whatever is necessary to live an authentic life.* Why? Because half-guided fantasies, half-realized dreams, and half-actions taken will ensure a life only half lived and a potential never realized.

The Ninja remained in their mist-shrouded mountain sanctuaries for hundreds of years. It was only in 1581 that the military ruler of Japan, General Nobunaga Oda, influenced by the growth and teachings of Christianity, struck against their mysticism and deliberately set out to destroy them. He required the brute force of a massive army to do so, outnumbering the Ninja men, women, and children by more than ten to one, and even then many Ninja survived, scattering themselves widely to avoid tracking and detection, and taking themselves deeper into hiding.

Over the course of these centuries, the practices of the Ninja approached a high art. And yet, Hoban reminds us, "Ninja were not wizards or witches, but ordinary men and women with a unique philosophical viewpoint. . . . *Ninpo* [the Way of Endurance], or the essence of the Ninja's outlook, is a physical, emotional, and spiritual method of self-protection from the dangers that confront those on the warrior path to enlightenment."[5]

The Ninja were, in fact, people just like us—searching for answers, aware of magnificent powers within themselves, aware of how these powers are so often trammelled and controlled by the systems of the world, but seeking nevertheless to transcend these limitations and be all they could be.

The key to success was the psychospiritual approach of the Ninja and not, as the movies portray, their fighting skills. The psychology of the Ninja—their inner preparation and purification—was the primary factor, because nothing at all can take place in the world without our first having a vision of what it is and what we intend it to achieve. Therefore, if you are studying Ninjutsu or any other martial art, you may find this book of value—but its real worth is in showing you how to apply warrior spirituality for greater effectiveness in the world, whether that amounts to better relationships or to making millions, in your personal assessment of what would make you most happy and free.

Ninja philosophy is entirely correct—and in psychological terms, clinically accurate—when it says that we must face our fears, find our power, apply this with vision, and deal with—rather than suppress—our problems, if we are to be fulfilled individuals. That is the message of this book, and the techniques it includes are geared toward that.

Of course, such a process is not unique to the Ninja; it is an underlying discipline of all warrior traditions. You will find parallels in this book with Toltec philosophy, with the heroic approach of the Celts, and with many other schools of thought. I have not shied away from including these other teachings where they are important to our journey, nor should you. After all, the Ninja themselves absorbed freely what was useful from like-minded traditions they encountered.

Underlying all of this is the truth of the *Amatsu Tatara* and the Ninja: *You can have anything you want*—if you *apply to your life* the principles and processes that you read about here. Just reading about them is not enough; it is their application that counts. That is our route to freedom and happiness.

The point is the doing of them. . . . There is no actor but the action; there is no experiencer but the experience.

—BRUCE LEE

ONE

The Initiation into Being: Boldness has Genius

Beginning the Journey of this Book

*Concerning all acts of initiative and creation, there is one ele-
mentary rule . . . that the moment one definitely commits oneself, then Providence moves too. All sorts of things occur to help
one that would never otherwise have occurred. . . .*

Boldness has genius, power, and magic in it. Begin it now.

—GOETHE

Many people see Ninjutsu or
Ninpo—the skills of the Ninja—as combat oriented, but in reality the
spiritual aspect is never far from the surface. Training emphasizes mental discipline and the exploration of consciousness and human potential. Students learn to channel energy *(ki)*—the Tao, or life force of the
universe—to overcome challenges just as much as they learn physical
techniques for defeating an opponent.

Ninjutsu training is an initiation, through levels of skill, into a different order of life, where combat, in fact, becomes an irrelevance. Students absorb energy-raising techniques and special *kamae* (postures)
and *tai sabaki* (movements) that direct spiritual and mental energies
into the body to deal with particular situations. They also learn breathwork *(kokyu waza)* and other practices that give them access to new

7

realms of power, such as *ninshiki waza* (sensory training to develop a "sixth sense"), *messo* or *mu* (meditation or "no-mind"), *mushin* (spirit renewal), and *menriki* (awareness training).

This description may seem esoteric, but the emphasis, in fact, is always on the practical—on experience, encounters, and getting things done—rather than appeals to higher powers, because none of these techniques are actually of much value unless they *work*. Certainly this was true in the harsh (historical and political, as well as geographic) terrain that the Ninja knew as home. They were, by necessity, a pragmatic people, mystical rather than religious or dogmatic, and central to their philosophy was the understanding that there *is* no higher power than the actualized human being who is the meeting place of the material and the divine.

As Masaaki Hatsumi, the thirty-fourth Ninja grandmaster wrote: "In *every* encounter or experience, there is the potential for gaining our enlightenment, the possibility of finding that one missing piece of the puzzle that brings about illumination. It is our own mind that determines the experience."[1] A modern-day writer, Ian McEwan, gets right to the point when he writes, "The actual, not the magical, should be the challenge."[2]

The branch of Ninjutsu that deals specifically with mental and spiritual artistry is known as the *kuji-kiri*. It is the discipline of drawing down energy from the universe and directing it in order to develop our capacity for:

Rin: The knowledge of self and the true nature of being

Kai: Awareness of our motivations (our real purpose or mission) beyond those of our socialization into a particular role or position

Jin: Intuition or greater attunement to ourselves and the world around us

Toh: Insight into our lives and true needs

Pyo: Personal power

Zen: Self-protection through spiritual, emotional, physical, and mental skills and insight through greater awareness (the latter known as *zazen*)

Sha: The ability to heal ourselves through the release of old
    behavior patterns that can lead to self-harm and self-limitation
    as well as damage to others, our environment, and, through
    unskillful actions, to the world in general

Retsu: Freedom

Sai: Self-actualization through the final realization of a power that
    is already ours

The kuji-kiri underlies everything we will do in this book, as we
focus on the enhancement of spiritual and psychological skills rather
than the martial arts of the warriors. *The Spiritual Practices of the Ninja*
is also, however, a book of initiation—the central plank of the Ninja
tradition—so let us look first at what initiation means, as this will be
key to our work.

Initiation

I have always had a passion for travel, for pushing the envelope, and, by
finding myself in the most out-of-the-way places among the most unusual people, for trying to discover what it means to be a human being,
alive in this world at this one unique moment in history. What is it that I
came here to do, and where should this journey take me next?

As an explorer in this way, I have undertaken initiations myself and
met other initiates from many different traditions. The extraordinary
thing is that all these initiates have seemed healthier, happier, and more
empowered than we Westerners, even those living in third-world countries where poverty, hunger, and social disorder were rife. By Western
standards, these people should have been weak and miserable, I guess—
but they were not.

Being a therapist and a healer, to me the contrast seemed even more
marked. My Western clients come from the richest countries on Earth
and often have good jobs and high standards of living. Yet they are des-
perately unhappy in one way or another. Many of them seek out my help
with existential problems of an emotional, mental, or spiritual nature,

or, just as often, and more vaguely (because they cannot even put a name to their problem), because they feel "lost" or "stuck." Those are words I have never heard among initiates in tribal societies. I began to wonder what these people have that we in the West do not.

What it came down to was this: the initiatory process itself. Every initiation offered an intense experience of empowerment and liberation, in the form of ritual challenges and exercises designed to test the initiate's courage, power, clarity of vision, and what we might call his or her "spirit" or "zest for living." These four—courage, power, clarity, and zest—are the Four Gates to Freedom that were well known to the Ninja from their own initiations (their walking on fire, their hanging from cliffs), and once the initiates passed through them, they became transformed and better able to take control of their lives.

Since we in the modern world no longer have such initiations, we never have the opportunity to pass through these gateways and so we remain stuck, experiencing only the negative or shadow sides of these four states—not courage but fear; not power but powerlessness; not clarity but confusion; and, in place of a natural zest for living, soul fatigue— a sort of existential boredom or giving up on life. These four shadows are our greatest enemies to love, liberation, and happiness.

The initiations of the Ninja in Japan, as well as those I encountered in other countries, brought every warrior face to face with these enemies. It might be the fear of stepping onto a path of hot coals that the initiate had to walk. It might be the powerlessness an initiate felt when told to do the seemingly impossible, such as to find an underwater cave containing a spiritual treasure of some kind.[3] It might be confusion at being told to leap into an abyss with the reassurance that it was okay, he would find he could fly![4] Or the arduousness, loneliness, and exertion of being sent out into the wilderness on a quest for vision or a burial in the earth.*

When I looked at these practices, I saw that the process of initiation was always based on reconnecting the young man or woman with the

---

*Malidoma Somé describes such an underwater quest as part of the African initiatory experience. The jump into the abyss was one of the initiations undertaken by Carlos Castaneda during his apprenticeship to the Yaqui shaman don Juan. Burial in the earth is an

elements: hot coals (Fire), river caves (Water), the leap into the abyss (Air), and the vision quest or burial ceremony (Earth).

The importance of the elements is reflected in the Ninja concept of the Godai, the five energies that make up all there is and which can be used in our quest for freedom.

Ka is the quality of Fire and corresponds to feelings of vitality, physicality, self-direction, and courage. It is the archetypal energy of the Lover—she who is in love with and passionate about life.* We get in touch with ka through the body.

Sui is the quality of Water and represents flexibility, adaptability, the ability to "go with the flow" and find balance and self-assurance. It is the energy of the Seeker—he who searches for answers and looks for his own source of power. We find our sui through the emotions.

Fu is the quality of Air and relates to wisdom, clarity, personal truth, self-reflection, and self-knowledge. It is the energy of the Magus, the person of vision who has found an individual and authentic way of being in the world. Discovering this within ourselves is the work of the clear and skillful mind.

Chi is the quality of Earth, which is experienced as a sense of stability, groundedness, spiritual maturity, and the capacity for happiness. It is the energy of the Soul Warrior, who is prepared to fight his battles on the field of the spirit to gain mastery of himself, instead of projecting his pain out into the world and creating the very chaos that causes suffering.

Finally, in the Godai, **Ku** is the place of the Void, the experience of self-actualization, naturalness of being, and attunement to all things, which the warrior will encounter once he has met the other

---

initiatory practice common to many warrior traditions, including those of Africa and North America. See notes section for sources of information on these initiatory practices.

*The Lover, Seeker, Magus, Soul Warrior, and Mystic are all archetypes, which are a means of giving the Godai elements a personality and identity in this book. The subject of archetypes is dealt with more fully in the next chapter.

elements and awoken their qualities in himself. It is the place of the Mystic, who has understood his position at the center of all things.

It is said that without initiation and practice, we cannot access these elemental and archetypal energies and so they remain uncontrolled, unused, or unnoticed. They can even work against us, which is the real problem we face. It is only when we draw them into consciousness that they become our allies.

Initiation kick-starts this process by reconnecting us with the power and excitement, the wonder and awe, of being alive. It is this—our new-found ability to appreciate the gifts of life, to face our challenges head on, and to deal with what is (rather than lose ourselves in a fantasy of how we'd like things to be)—that makes us awake, aware, and fully involved in the life we are living. Initiation introduces us to the world as it really is, with all of its beauty and mystery, hardship and hope. It allows us to discover who we are and what we might be capable of, and to prove ourselves as men and women of power.

A World without Meaning

So hungry are we for initiatory rites in a modern world that offers us so few of them that we are inclined to make up our own rituals, sometimes with disastrous consequences. Robert Moore and Douglas Gillette write of the "pseudo-rituals" of our culture, such as the violence and humiliation of inductions into college fraternities or street gangs, which may in some cases involve ritual murder in order for the would-be member to "prove" himself. Another example is the induction into "families" such as the Mafia, where two candidates for membership are taken into the desert and, at gunpoint, dig their own graves. One of them may then be shot and buried—the other, by implication, having "made it," though the choice is often arbitrary. Death and rebirth are at the heart of many initiatory experiences, though rarely so literally, so brutally, or with so little point.

The result of such toxic rituals is that those who go through them become "skewed, stunted, and false . . . abusive of others, and often of self."[5] This, the authors contend, is at the root of many of our social problems and has created a society that is concerned only with "the struggle for dominance of others." If we have no rituals to guide us, we can find ourselves lost and without ethics, unsure of what to do apart from trying to steal the power of others, one of the things our Western upbringing has taught us to do well (see Eli's story in chapter 6).

In a culture where controlled and purposeful initiations, such as those practiced by the Ninja, are lacking, there is little chance for us to gain mastery of our energies because there is no opportunity, challenge, or encouragement to do so. Since these energies are therefore unfocused and undirected, they can all too easily flip into their shadow sides—fear, powerlessness, confusion, and soul fatigue—leading to the problems we face today.*

In my therapeutic practice I meet the casualties of this system: people who grew up without real mothers and fathers to give them the attention, love, and education they needed, because they, in turn, had never been initiated into power nor learned what is important in life; nor what their own children might need in order to grow up with a sense of well-being, integrity, and self-direction. Many have been so concerned with their own dramas and unresolved issues that they have created a life of power games and misery for their children instead, if for no other reason than to stop feeling so powerless and alone themselves—a sort of "comfort in numbers and misery."

---

*"Turning eighteen is the milestone birthday that traditionally marks the passage from adolescence to adulthood. But it seems many of us are taking much longer to really grow up," writes Stephanie Condron in the *Daily Mail,* August 2, 2004 ("The Over-18s With a Lot of Growing Up to Do"). Citing research in the UK and the United States that applied different tests of adulthood, such as leaving home and becoming financially independent, she reports that "the teenage years seem to be stretching well into the 30s" and "fewer 30-year-olds can really be considered adults." The research shows that in 1960, 65 percent of males and 70 percent of females over 18 could be regarded as having passed the tests for adulthood. Nowadays, the figures are 46 percent and 25 percent, respectively. The study she quotes (led by Professor Frank Furstenberg, a sociologist at the University of Pennsylvania) concludes that "adulthood no longer begins where adolescence ends." Making this transition is precisely the point of initiation in traditional societies.

We have become adults who do not know who we are; in some ways, we are still children, looking for answers from wisdom-keepers who do not exist. We do not know how to meet our needs—at times we don't even know what these needs are—or how to live in a correct and fulfilling way. Increasingly our world is one of absent parents and children with no real adult role models. Our education focuses on what it means to be an "expert" or a functionary—doctor, electrician, engineer—and not a well-rounded human being. Even our religious institutions have become businesses, many of which have no place for the spirit and some of which are discredited and in decline. It is no wonder that we suffer "soul loss"—a massive disconnection from ourselves and the living world.

In our "flattened lives," as Herbert Marcuse described them, our men are taught to operate from their heads and bodies and to ignore their spirituality and emotions; our women are taught to be emotional (often overly so) and perhaps even "spiritual" but ashamed of their bodies and intellect. We are fractured individuals, divided as men and women who cannot understand the needs and motivations of each other, looking for completion by chasing the material symbols of having "made it." But made what exactly? Who are we, and where are we going?

The rituals of the Ninja and other traditional societies answer these questions. Through ceremony and trials of courage, they bring out the real men in their boys, the real women in their girls, and create people of power and knowledge who have graduated into wholeness.

So important is this function of initiation that in some societies, these challenges are extreme. Dr. Geo Trevarthen writes of Australian initiatory practices, for example, that "Everyone doesn't pass them or live through them in some cases. There's a photo of initiands lying in a semicircle after they've been put through parts of their initiation. Some of them have white markers next to them. These are the ones who are dead. This is what Aborigines would do to get their power."[6]

This book offers you an opportunity for initiation into courage, power, clarity about your life, and the zest to live it fully. Your journey will not be as extreme as that described by Trevarthen, of course, but it *will* be challenging, and you should read it as if your life depended on it.

Because, in a way, it does—if we mean conscious life, the awareness of who we are or want to be. It does, if we want to act with authenticity, integrity, and, most of all, with choice and free will—to *truly* live, that is, instead of doing what we are told.

The Processes and Techniques of This Book

All initiations have three stages:

First there is a descent into mystery—a time of unknowing. This is when initiates leave the past behind, letting go of their illusions and the things that no longer serve them. It is a time of separation from the known and normal and an opening up to limitless possibilities. In Ninja clans this was inherent because the children had already been taken out of consensus society and lived among nature in the Iga and Koga mountains, where the influence of mainstream thinking was less intensely felt. These *genin*—"untrained" or "small"—Ninja would be tutored from birth in a different order of reality. We are not so lucky and have to unlearn much of what we have been taught about the way to live. This initiatory stage began for you the minute you started to question your life enough to pick up this book.

Next comes the warrior's challenge, a time for facing fears, tackling the obstacles to growth, and proving oneself through action—because "awareness" is one thing but living consciously and *acting* from a place of integrity and power is quite another. Knowledge is nothing without application, for, as Casteneda's Yaqui shaman said, "One learns to act like a warrior by acting, not by talking."[7] The child-Ninja would be offered challenges from birth to test his spiritual, mental, and physical acuity. Once again, it is unlikely that any of us were given such an opportunity to stand in our power and on our own two feet, but the exercises in this book offer you that challenge.

Finally, there is the homecoming, a celebration of the newborn men and women—kings and queens of personal destiny who have achieved mastery of the self and experienced the magic of an awakened life. For the Ninja, this meant an opportunity for elevation to the rank of *chunin*, or middle Ninja—a person who had faced his fears and proven himself worthy to come under the guidance of a *jonin,* or high Ninja—a tribal chief as we might say today. Your commitment to the exercises in this book give you the opportunity to arrive at this place psychologically, if you are ready to accept the challenges they present.

Actually, this process is as much about remembering who you are and the work you came here to do as it is about gaining new abilities, for the Ninja believe that we all have our power within us, as our birthright. The real initiation, then, is simply to remember who we are.

> *Remember you are all people and all people are you.*
> *Remember you are this universe and this universe is you.*
>
> —JOY HARJO

The techniques we will be working with in this book are derived from actual Ninja practices, informed by my therapeutic work and my experience of Ninja training but modernized for a Western audience. They also reflect the Godai and its focus on achieving balance through the harmonization of the internal elements of the body, emotions, mind, and spirit—Fire, Water, Air, and Earth.

These techniques include:

Thoughtwork. This is often just a case of asking the right questions, realizing that we create our own realities, so that everything we have in our lives (whether it serves us well or not) somehow comes back to a choice we have made. Most of these choices are unconscious; therefore, skillful thinking involves making our choices conscious . . . and knowing we can change them. We have that choice too.

Breathwork. One of the secrets of Ninjutsu (in fact, one of the most ancient and enduring practices of most spiritual traditions), and one of the most important keys to ourselves, is work with the breath. Every time you breathe in, you take in natural energy that is charged with your personal intention. While some traditions call it chi or prana—to the Ninja it was ki—all believe that if you are stuck with limiting beliefs about yourself and the world, you will breathe in further restrictions through your (unconscious) intention to do so and therefore feed (and so replicate) the self-limiting patterns you have become used to. The energy you take in with the breath is channeled through the filter of *who you believe you are* and directed into giving you more of the same. Once these patterns are broken, anything may be possible.

Visualization. This enables us to see the world and ourselves from a wholly different perspective, one that is richer and more holistic than the limited viewpoint most of us take for granted. When we do so, we realize that there is a world of possibilities open to us, not just one narrow path we must always walk.

Body movement and action. Our focus in the West is on the mind. We are good thinkers, but not great doers. Thinking is the way of stagnation and analysis (a compulsion to "over-stand" instead of understand the world), while real change comes from action, sensation, and experience. Simply by moving—doing something—we create new ways of connecting with the world and release some of our blockages and inhibitions. You will therefore encounter moving meditations, qi-gong-like techniques, and Ninja kamae for moving purposefully in the world during your reading of this book.

Practical creativity. Most of us have had the joy of personal creativity knocked out of us from an early age, most obviously in school where we were "streamed" as either "artists" or "scientists" as a result of someone else's judgments or definitions. Even if we were imprisoned in definition A and therefore granted more access to our creativity, we still had to create as "artists" in the officially approved way that enabled us to pass exams and gain a piece of paper, instead of creating as an expression of our passion and soul. True creativity is a rebellion against orthodoxy (the Ninja Way) and is in itself a gesture toward power and freedom. In this book you are therefore invited to use song, chanting, painting, writing, or whatever else grabs you as a vehicle of your own pure expression. So every time you read an instruction to "write down" your observations, feel free to ignore it and do something else that is more "you" instead. Paint or draw your insights, dance or sing them if you prefer.

Commitments. At various stages in this book, you will have an opportunity to interact with the material (assuming you agree with it), by making a commitment as an anchor for your decision to live differently.

Commitments are life affirming and power enhancing. Most people set their own limitations. Offered an opportunity, they turn it down—because they don't feel they deserve it, feel guilty about taking it, think there must be a catch, allow themselves to believe they don't have the resources to make the best of it, or a million other reasons. As an experiment during my psychology degree, I once stood on a street corner and tried handing out five-pound notes (about $10)—free money—to passers-by. I began with £100 and returned home with £80 still in my pocket. As part of the experiment, an assistant caught up with all those who'd refused the money and asked them why. It turned out that most people thought there was something wrong with me, or with them, because free money was "just too good to be true."

We will never achieve anything if we remain hung up over such hang-ups. Energy is the life force of the universe. It is what keeps things going. By denying ourselves the opportunities we deserve and which are freely presented to us, we block the flow of this energy and turn our backs on these gifts from the universe. I suggest, therefore, that you make the commitments offered in this book, and stick to them. They are commitments not to me, but to yourself—the *you* that you have every right to be.

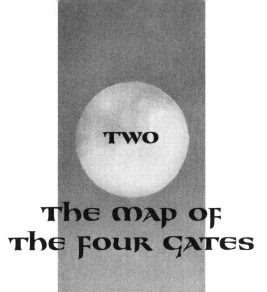

TWO

The Map of
The Four Gates

*You have no more time for retreats or for regret. You only have
time to live like a warrior.*

—DON JUAN IN *THE TEACHINGS OF DON JUAN*
BY CARLOS CASTANEDA

You are about to embark on a jour-
ney and, of course, every traveler needs a map. The map of the Four
Gates is an archetypal one, derived from a combination of Ninja practices and current psychological techniques to make these practices relevant and useful in a modern context.

It looks like the diagram on page 20.

At the cardinal points (east, south, west, and north) are the archetypal energies represented by the Godai. These are the forces or inner
powers that we must master as we make our journey through life, in
order to be our authentic selves.

In the Godai, these are the energies known as ka (Fire), sui (Water),
fu (Air), chi (Earth), and ku (Void). In this book, however, we will call
them by different names, in order to get more of a sense of their true
essence and of the archetypal forces behind them. These descriptions
will give us a feeling of what it is like to be in touch with these elements
of the Godai.

19

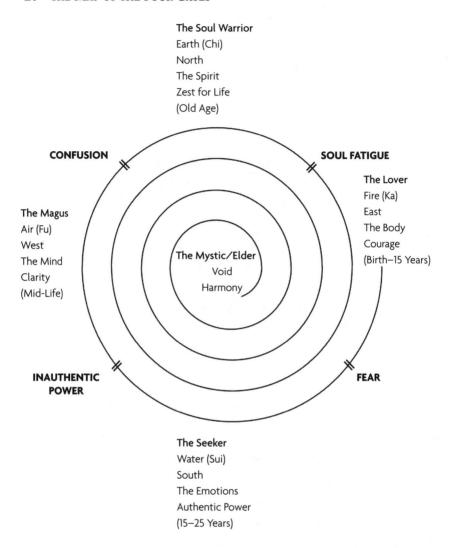

The Soul Warrior
Earth (Chi)
North
The Spirit
Zest for Life
(Old Age)

CONFUSION

SOUL FATIGUE

The Lover
Fire (Ka)
East
The Body
Courage
(Birth–15 Years)

The Magus
Air (Fu)
West
The Mind
Clarity
(Mid-Life)

The Mystic/Elder
Void
Harmony

INAUTHENTIC POWER

FEAR

The Seeker
Water (Sui)
South
The Emotions
Authentic Power
(15–25 Years)

Ka, then, is the Lover, suggesting the passion and fiery determination of this energy; sui is the Seeker, representing a flowing quality of movement seeking purpose; fu is the Magus, the magical power of the mind to create dramatic and material change; chi is the Soul Warrior, the steadfast power of the warrior and of the Earth to endure, no matter what; ku is the Mystic, the energy which allows us to connect with the essence of all things, known to the Ninja as the Void. In this chapter, we look at each of these archetypes in detail.

At the noncardinal points of the map are the gateways to transformation we must pass through so we can achieve these states of mastery. To get through each gateway is a rite of passage in itself, a minor initiation within the overall process, and each represents a challenge we all must face before our homecoming. As we pass through, we become ever more self-aware and gain greater control of our energies, emotions, and mental states. We begin to exercise a conscious choice over our destinies, and through that choice we move toward freedom.

Lover, Seeker, Magus, Soul Warrior, Mystic: The Five Archetypal Energies

The term *archetype* was used by the Swiss psychoanalyst Carl Jung to describe a "preconscious psychic disposition that enables a man [or woman] to react in a human manner."[1] Our archetypes serve as a mythological "way of being human," a model of behavior woven into the twilight stories of parents to their children down through the ages. Not only do these stories still exist in myths, legends, and fairy tales, but the energy of their repeated telling gives them a life of their own, which is absorbed into the collective unconscious, the pool of energetic thought from which all things come. For the Ninja, the human spirit is a traveler from this pool of thought (the Void) before it becomes flesh and we are born as children, and so we ourselves are infused with these same mythic qualities and archetypal energies.

Archetypes have a resonance in the soul of every human being. Jung found the same basic stories and images in every culture and period of human history and concluded that this was because human beings do not just have separate and unique minds, but also a share in the universal mind, where all experiences and life stories can be found.

Our problem as human beings is that these bigger stories from the universal mind can sometimes become more powerful to us than our own living reality, at which point we begin to act out a dream instead of being who we are. In a time of war, for example, our governments are adept at promoting the myth of the archetypal hero as one who lays down his or her life for God and Country, and many a young man (or woman) is sucked into this drama, losing his life to a dream, without even questioning his support for this war or whether he is really ready to die. He has become the myth itself.

The Ninja knew about archetypes more than twelve hundred years before Jung developed the concept. The Ninja did not, of course, use this term themselves, but they had a sense of humanity's mythological connection to the spirit of all things. One word that captures this is *aiki*—"internal spirit"—which carries a suggestion of an energy and way of acting in the world that is informed and empowered by a universal force.

Recognizing the human tendency to believe in stories more often than the things we see with our own eyes, the Ninja became masters of myth and deception by employing archetypes to their advantage.* Thus, the Ninja knew that an enemy soldier, seeing an old man in a dirty robe carrying a staff and bowl, would notice only a wandering beggar, his mind creating the rest of the story and inventing an entire back history and mythology to account for the old man, when in reality a young warrior stood before him in disguise. By presenting an easy picture in this way, the Ninja were able to make ingress into many enemy strongholds, discover their secrets and strategies, and then vanish into the night, the enemy having been caught off guard by a single old beggar when they had expected an attack from an entire Ninja clan.

Similarly, the techniques of the female Ninja included training in the skills of love (*kunoichijutsu*—the "art of the deadly flower") so she could operate effectively as a courtesan, allowing her to get close to an enemy general without detection. He saw only a beautiful and adoring young woman, while in reality she would also have been trained in the warrior arts of espionage, combat, and poisoning.

---

*The Ninja's techniques of infiltration and subterfuge were well developed and relied on such practices. Some examples are *genjutsu*—the art of illusion; *intonjutsu*—the art of disappearance; *chika iri*—deception at close range; *hensogakurejutsu*—the use of disguise to blend with the environment; *youjang no jutsu*—information gathering; *gisojutsu*—the art of impersonation; and *shibagakurejutsu*—"hiding in nature's cloak."

Once we understand the concept of archetypes, we can apply their energy to achieve any number of objectives in the world. Archetypes are not just a means to deception, however; they are real energies within us. Many of us will be living their mythological stories quite unconsciously, acting in the world as if we really are the person we have come to believe we are as a result of the story we have accepted or invented about ourselves. In this way, we do not see the full range of our potential but instead live out the myth we have been socialized into. We do not call upon our natural abilities because we do not know they exist. To make these energies conscious and to master the powers they give us is the task of the initiatory journey.

There are, of course, numerous archetypes that cover the human story.* We can see the influence of archetypes within the three classic Viennese schools of psychotherapy. Freud, for example, based his theory of human development around the "pleasure principle" (also known as the will to pleasure), which is the archetypal energy I have called the Lover, the passion represented by Fire (ka) in the Ninja Godai. Adler spoke of "striving for superiority"—or the will to power—which is the Seeker's quest (sui). Frankl wrote of the will to meaning, which is the concern of the Magus (fu). Jung, of course, wrote more about archetypes than anyone else, and was primarily concerned with them as a source of inner knowing. This is the field of the Soul Warrior (chi) and the Mystic (ku). According to the Godai, the qualities embodied by the Lover, Seeker, Magus, Soul Warrior, and Mystic are the most resonant and enduring. These five energies are what give structure to life's journey. So let us explore them in a little detail and see how they impact our lives.

---

*Caroline Myss, in her book *Sacred Contracts* (New York: Bantam, 2002), lists more than seventy archetypes: Advocate, Artist, Beggar, Bully, Destroyer, Detective, Femme Fatale, Gambler, and so on. Also see www.myss.com/ThreeArchs.asp. These reduce to twelve primary archetypes in her model, all of which "play valuable roles that relate to our work, our relationships with individuals and society, as well as to our spirituality, finances, values, and our highest potential." Robert Moore also looks at archetypes, primarily from the perspective of the men's movement. See *King, Warrior, Magician, Lover: Rediscovering the Archetypes of the Mature Masculine* (San Francisco: Harper, 1991).

The Lover

The lover's world is different from ours. In the world of lovers there is no gain and there is no loss, there is only love and intoxication, which always comes with true love.

—SYED HAMRAZ AHSAN

Element:	Fire (ka)
Experienced through:	Physical sensations
Exploration of the world through:	The body
Aim of the Lover:	Connection
The Lover's gift:	Courage
Ninja principle used to reveal this gift:	*Tai sabaki* ("body movement" or "body truth")
Gateway:	Fear
Shadow:	Wounded Lover or Heroic Failure
Manifestation of the shadow:	Chaos or control
Chronological age:	Birth to age fifteen
Stage of the journey:	Beginning

Looking again at the map on page 20, you will see that we are born in the east of the spiral, bringing with us the energy of the Lover. East is the direction of awareness and connection with all things, before we have yet heard the stories and myths that will come to define and limit us. This original state of being is exemplified by the joy, passion, and vigor of young children who throw themselves fully and excitedly into life, engaging with and exploring this new world of mystery and adventure they are a part of.

The Lover is delighted at this amazing new playground he has been born into and his greatest tool for exploring it is his body—physical sensation and feeling—an endless source of joy for the child who is able to run, sing, dance, and play freely in ways we adults forget. This passion and excitement of the child at play is represented by the element of Fire (ka).

What the Lover has (and which some of us quickly come to lose if our upbringing and life experiences do not support it) is a natural courage, fearlessness, the ability to just *be*, and a desire to explore and connect with people and things around him. If we can keep our passionate child alive in ourselves, we will grow into lovers of life who delight in adventure and new encounters, are at ease in meeting new people, exploring new situations and sensations, confident in the world, and happy with our bodies.

Mastery of this state means facing our first initiatory challenge—fear—and passing it. Normally, this challenge will present itself before the age of fifteen (in tribal societies, formal initiations for boys and girls often take place at thirteen). For Ninja children, however, training to meet these challenges might begin soon after birth, with gentle exercises and *maneru shimei* (mock assignments presented as games) to turn the *kusa* (literally, "little weeds"—Ninja without formal training) into *monjin* (disciples of the art).

Since we in the West no longer set formal challenges for our young, these days it is life itself that provides the tests. All children are exposed to the fears, hopes, and anxieties of their parents and will absorb the fears of the world around them through socialization into its ways of life, accepting this as natural and adapting themselves to it. Their challenge is to break free of this imposed description of the world so they can still see it as their adventure playground and engage with it joyfully. Without formal initiation, however, it is difficult for children to even recognize that a test is being set for them, that this worldview is not the only one and that they do not have to accept its fears and lack of freedom.

If, because of this socialization, they cannot accept their first initiatory challenge (and thus they fail to meet it), they may grow into frightened adults themselves—shy, withdrawn, angry, sad, and unable to connect with others. They may also feel a sense of shame, confusion, or dislike for their bodies and may believe (as is the case with anorexics, for example) that they must control them lest they themselves are overpowered. Or perhaps they give up the natural connection to their bodies and give in to addictions where they are controlled by a substance instead.

These shadow responses of control or chaos are unhealthy reactions that result from not facing their first challenge and walking through the gateway of fear so they can master their Lover's energy.

In psychological terms, we tend to act out from our shadow sides if we are not in touch with a particular inner state. "Acting out" is the uncontrolled and sometimes violent release of unconscious thoughts or feelings, often by projecting them onto others and then acting as if these others are responsible for them. So, for example, if we have a fear of intimacy (because of an unsatisfactory relationship with our mothers, or because we feel abandoned by our fathers, etc.), it is often easier to stay in our comfort zone of Wounded Lover or Heroic Failure, unlucky in love—the shadows of the Lover—rather than face our fears and allow ourselves to be vulnerable before others, in case they hurt us too. And so we carry our fears of abandonment into future relationships and choose men or women who in some way remind us of our fathers or mothers. Then, through our behavior, we create the very scenario of abandonment we have already experienced and unconsciously most fear. This is our shadow at play.

Because we fear abandonment, we may become control freaks or jealous lovers, for example, to the extent that our partners eventually do leave us. We can then return to our comfort zones and become abandoned children once again, having proven to ourselves that intimacy really is something to be feared.

This shadow play is a way of acting out our inner state of terror. But the thing that really holds us back is our inability to face our first enemy, fear: the fear of being real, of doing things in a different, nonhabitual, way, of stepping outside our comfort zones and making a success of our lives. This is, in fact, a form of madness, which Einstein defined perfectly as doing the same things in the same way and expecting a different outcome at the end of it.

Because of the chaos and turmoil such shadow plays can create, initiations always include an element of controlled fear so that the shadow is brought into the light of the initiate's mind and that particular gateway can be crossed.

Fear is the most important gateway, because without the boost of energy that comes from releasing our fears, we will find it difficult to go on with the rest of the journey. For this reason it is given the most attention in this book. The way to master fear is to know the truth of the body (tai sabaki), as we shall see.

The Seeker

All truths are easy to understand once they are discovered; the point is to discover them.

—GALILEO GALILEI

Element:	Water (sui)
Experienced through:	Purpose
Exploration of the world through:	The emotions
Aim of the Seeker:	Personal power
The Seeker's gift:	Authentic power
Ninja principle used to reveal this gift:	*Kodawari* (freeing ourselves from emotional fixations)
Gateway:	Inauthentic power
Shadow:	Victim/Martyr or Drone
Manifestation of the shadow:	Takes power from others or allows it to be taken
Chronological age:	Fifteen to twenty-five
Stage of the journey:	First steps on the path (early days in any endeavor)

If our initiation through fear into Lover energy is successful, the next archetype we will meet is the Seeker (in the south of the spiral). The adventuring spirit of the Lover is now coming to fruition. The Seeker is an explorer, searching for answers to life's questions and a direction and purpose of his own.

The search may be that of a spiritual or scientific adventurer or a confident traveler who delights in visiting new countries, tasting new cultures, and meeting new people; or it may appear far more mundane than that—someone trying to find his niche in life, a good job, or advancement in a career. Underlying all of this, however, the search is always existential or metaphysical: "Why am I here?" "What is my role and purpose?" "What is the meaning of this life *for me?*" The genuine Seeker—overjoyed by the excitement of the quest—is happy just to be in this game of life, intrigued by the questions, and wholeheartedly into the challenge. He or she may hope to find "the Truth" as an outcome to the puzzle, or to win the game in some way, but these competitive drives are not what bring the Seeker joy, per se: it is being in the mystery with so much to explore. That is why he is playing the game at all—for the fun of it.

There may come a time, however, when the Seeker becomes frustrated or dispirited because he cannot find the answers he is looking for. Usually this is because he is looking in the wrong place—in the world *out there* instead of the world within, which is vaster and rich with answers if he only knew how and where to look. This requires initiation into authentic power, so that such hard-to-come-by knowledge can be found.

Without this initiation our Seekers might never find their answers and may fall instead into their shadow selves. Two common modern shadows of the Seeker are the Drone and the Victim/Martyr. The former is characteristic of the person who has accepted the social definition of power and now finds himself a functionary in a job, a marriage, or a lifestyle taken on because that is what is expected of him, and not as the result of a conscious choice. He lacks *shiki* (a resolute spirit), in other words, and is living a social myth instead of a personal truth.

The Drone will intuit this lack of true power and may respond by trying to take it from others, becoming a domineering boss or a demanding wife, for example, both of whom may appear strong and resourceful—even successful—but are actually lost and unhappy in their knowledge of a life and a promise unlived.

The other response of the powerless Seeker is to become a Victim/Martyr, someone for whom life is a drab, meaningless place that has never given her anything. The Victim may also respond to her lot by seeking to take energy, power, and answers from others to fill the hole in her own life.

One of my students, Pansy, had fallen into this role. Her search was for the perfect soul mate, a man who could complete her and make her whole; someone, in other words, who could give her power to compensate for the things she felt lacking in herself. Inspired by the romanticism of Joseph Campbell, Pansy saw herself as a princess at the center of a drama and spoke of her ideal lover as a knight on a quest to rescue her, to "tame the perilous bed . . . the woman's temperament," and so gain his "just rewards"—her.

Pansy was referring to Joseph Campbell's retelling of an old warrior myth where the hero must spend a night on a "perilous bed" in order to win the affection of a "fair maiden." The bed is in turmoil and the hero is assaulted by poisoned arrows, attacked by a thug, and mauled by a lion throughout the night. In the morning, having survived his trials, the hero is greeted by the maiden, who considers his courage and rewards him appropriately (in her opinion!), according to her "merci." In its original form the myth is a warning against the dangers that mindless or irresponsible love (or lust) can lead us all into. Pansy's version, however, seemed to be a warning specifically to men of how easy it can be to give away power to a woman in return for something ephemeral (the promise of true and unconditional love—defined in her terms, of course, and with all of her conditions attached!), which she may never be able to deliver because of her fascination (in warrior terms) with her own self-importance. This is a condition known to the Ninja as *kisha*.

When she wrote this to me, Pansy had just emerged from yet another in a long line of failed relationships with "unsuitable" men. This was her pattern: to leave her lovers when she realized they had no power to give her and that, ultimately, she would have to find her own power in herself. Instead of doing so, she would simply move on to the next man, hoping to find her answers in him.

Pansy was angered by this latest failure, this lack of a romantic ending to the drama she had created—her mythic quest for wholeness—and was set on preventing her ex-lover from seeing the son they had had together. Unconsciously she assumed that everyone around her should suffer because she was in pain. Of course, this shadow play merely invited further suffering, since the father was proposing legal action to gain access to his son, a case he would inevitably win, and Pansy would be even more frustrated and hurt.*

Pansy was invoking self-sabotage and the reinforcement of her Victim role, as she seemed intent on prolonging her drama by directing her energies into a new quest: the control of her newborn son, who was even more vulnerable and powerless than she, but who would naturally grow up to resent his mother for her attempt to control his life once he was aware of the truth. The healing for Pansy was to go inward, to connect with her pain, and not to direct it outward onto others so she never had to look at herself.

As Pansy's story suggests, the Seeker's motivation is really a quest for power. The problem is that we cannot obtain power through possession—not of a son, a sports car, or an unconditional love—even though, mistakenly, the will to possess is often how we define power in the West.

Authentic power is found in emotional mastery. We find power in *being* happy, not by owning things or people that we hope will *make* us happy. (This, in fact, is giving away our power by investing it in something outside ourselves and giving that thing control over our personal happiness.) Power is an internal quality, which we must find and call into consciousness. No one can tell the Seeker, "Yes, you have found the answer, now move on in your journey." We have to feel it for ourselves and know in our hearts that we have discovered our meaning and purpose.

Because of this connection to the emotions, Seeker energy is sym-

---

*Legal issues aside, a person who behaves in such a way by dragging a child (or anyone else) into his or her own drama, will always lose in at least two fundamental ways. First, by trying to "claim ownership" of the child and treat him as "property" in a game of revenge, he or she merely alienates the child further and will eventually lose him, no matter what, since no one wants to be treated as a possession. Second, by acting from bitterness, one reinforces his or her own illness and the negative patterns become self-perpetuating. Such a life becomes one of further loss. As it turned out, Pansy also lost the legal case as well, making her a three-time loser.

bolized by the element of Water (sui), which embodies the ability to flow with life, to access the deep unconscious, and to retain a center of balance, an even keel, despite the rises and falls, the ebbs and flows of life. It is represented by the Ninja discipline of *kodawari*—the strategy of learning our truth by freeing ourselves from emotional fixations and confused feelings about ourselves and our lives.

Chronologically, the age of seeking comes into focus in the teens to mid-twenties, when issues of power and finding our way become central to our lives. Of course, we are not talking just about age with any of these stages; you may well be forty-five and still looking for answers, for power, for emotional balance. (Pansy was thirty.) Teens to twenties, however, is typically when we seek to put frameworks in place and set up our lives according to the answers we have found to be "true"—so far, at least.

The gateway for our initiation into Seeker energy is overcoming *inauthentic* power. If we can understand what true power is and step into it, we will find our purpose and achieve our peace. We may then meet the next archetypal aspect of our selves—the Magus.

The Magus

The truth is what is, *not what* should be. *What should be* is a dirty lie.

—LENNY BRUCE

Element:	Air (fu)
Experienced through:	Vision
Exploration of the world through:	Mental artistry
Aim of the Magus:	Understanding
The Magus's gift:	Clarity
Ninja principle used to reveal this gift:	*Honshin* (true mind) or *kyojutsu ten kan* (approaching truth as though it were deception and deception as though it were truth)

Gateway:	Confusion
Shadow:	Manipulator or Bewildered Man or Woman
Manifestation of the shadow:	Blindness or arrogance
Chronological age:	Mid-life
Stage of the journey:	The middle

The Magus (in the west of the spiral) is the wizard, the person of vision and clarity, who understands who he is and his place in the world, and can act with consciousness, courage, and authentic power. He or she retains the Lover's passion and the Seeker's spirit of adventure, but now he has a clear vision in life as well, so his energies can be focused to achieve what he wills and not squandered on fruitless searches and misguided missions.

The Magus is a technician of the mind and a master of change and transformation. In traditional societies he or she may be the shaman, witch doctor, or medicine man. To the Ninja he was known as the *mahotsukai* (the magician), a person who saw into both worlds: the physical and the spiritual (those things—the emotions, the unconscious, our empathic communion with others—that also guide our interactions with the world), and could draw from both in order to clarify the unknowns of life.

The key word here is *vision*. The Magus is a visionary, a master of information, inspiration, and application of these qualities to the business of living. His greatest tool is the clear mind *(honshin)*, which sees through ego games (his own as well as others') and is able to get to the truth. This necessitates the questioning of "reality" and the realization that any "truth" is merely a description of the world that one can choose to accept or not. This is the meaning of *kyojutsu ten kan:* looking upon the truth as if it were, in fact, a deception—a socially constructed myth—and upon deception (the alternatives to this myth) as if it were equally true.

The Magus is also aware of another concept, that of service. He or she understands that we are all in some way connected; that every change we make has repercussions, like ripples in a pond, for everyone we are in contact with. If he lives correctly and is true to what he knows, the vision of the Magus itself becomes an act of service, a message to others and an inspiration for them.

Without initiation into this energy, we can fall prone to its shadow in two ways. We become Manipulators who think we have all the answers and can impose them on others so that *they* live *our* lives as well (a situation well known to the Ninja, who were subject to a number of repressive regimes), or we become the Bewildered, the fragmented people who begin to question their own vision, so their whole foundation for living can vanish overnight.

We can see a clear example of the Manipulator today in cult leaders. Many start as powerful and charismatic individuals who seem to have found a new truth for themselves, one that might also benefit others. And, indeed, perhaps they have, perhaps it would. Their challenge—and their failure—comes when others are drawn to them to learn this truth, and rather than passing it on they impose rules of living over these others. Their rules lock their acolytes into a system of belief instead of honoring the quest they are on and recognizing the unique contributions of the individual. Acolytes reinforce the vision of the shadow Magi ("I cannot be wrong. Look at all these people who agree with me!") and help assuage their own self-doubt.

For the same reason, the shadow Magi may become not cult leaders, but "experts," spokespersons, politicians, chiefs, or even authors—people who use their position to control a viewpoint, a worldview, a country, or a world, and mold it to their personal vision to convince themselves they are right. Such leaders may be benign or be malign, but they are always dictators. What they are effectively saying is, "This is my truth and it *will* be yours."

The other manifestation of the shadow Magus is the confused or bewildered man or woman, who cannot make sense of the world at all. Kevin was a client who exemplified this. He was engaged to Tracy, but their relationship was at best shaky, and he was struggling to get a handle on why.

Kevin was aware of Tracy's issues around trust, her fear of commitment and responsibility, and her willingness to run away when the going got tough in their relationship. But he had always taken her back when, a few days after she ran from whatever problems they were currently having, she had called and asked to come home again.

Kevin came to see me the third time Tracy left, because this time felt different: he didn't want her back. This puzzled him, because he thought he loved her and was willing to take his commitments seriously. But now he also recognized something in himself: he had been *playing the role* of an understanding lover, when actually he didn't like her much at all!

Through our healing work, Kevin was able to let go of his guilt about this and realize that any blame for the failure of the relationship was not his to bear alone and, in fact, he'd have needed the patience of a saint to put up with Tracy's behavior! With this realization he was able to step into a new sense of power and a new vision for his future.

No sooner had Kevin realized this than Tracy called and asked to come back again. Kevin declined the offer this time and eventually found a new partner who is more aligned to his own life's journey.

In the words of the philosopher Howard Thurman: "There are two questions a man must ask himself: The first is 'Where am I going?' and the second is 'Who will go with me?' If you ever get these questions in the wrong order you are in trouble."[2]

The initiatory challenge of the Magus, then, is to overcome confusion. The Magus must use the tool of the mind in skillful thinking so he can look clearly at his life and find a real vision for it. If he cannot do so he runs the risk, like Kevin, of meeting his shadow self: the Bewildered one who allows other people or a sense of guilt or uncertainty to control him because he does not retain clarity over who he is.

Magus energy is symbolized by the Godai element of Air (fu), the clear wind that blows away the fog of confusion and brings us a view of distant horizons and a sense of rejuvenation. It is represented by the Ninja arts of *satsujinjutsu* (the study of the mind and how it affects our internal battles) and *kokoro gamae* (techniques of mental clarity), both of which lead to *kageshin*—the quiet mind, freed from confusion and aggression toward the self and others.

In chronological terms, Magus energy will normally present in middle life. It is the time of the "mid-life (healing) crisis," when we re-evaluate our lives, re-envision our present, and put our energies into reinventing the future. If we can achieve mastery of this energy, then we approach the next step of the journey and gain access to the archetype that will guide us into the future: that of the Soul Warrior.

The Soul Warrior

One's first step in wisdom is to question everything—and one's last is to come to terms with everything

— GEORG CHRISTOPH LICHTENBERG

Element:	Earth (chi)
Experienced through:	Laughter and silence
Exploration of the world through:	Spirituality and wisdom
Aim of the Soul Warrior:	Balance and reconnection
The Soul Warrior's gift:	Zest for living
Ninja principle used to reveal this gift:	*Kiai* (focused and sustained internal energy)
Gateway:	Soul fatigue
Shadow:	Poor-me/Cynic
Manifestation of the shadow:	Escape into fantasy
Chronological age:	Elder/old age
Stage of the journey:	Ending

Having passed the initiatory tests to this point, the Soul Warrior (in the north of the spiral) has access to the fearlessness and passion of the Lover, the power of the Seeker, and the clarity and vision of the Magus. He is a person at one with his life mission.

For the self-realized man or woman who attains this level of mastery, there are only two proper responses to the game of life. One is laughter—at the joy and beauty of the world (which, despite its apparent failings, is all we have), and at how our petty concerns get in the way of our experience of every living moment. Each moment, after all, is an adventure; not the huge drama we have built it up to be, but an engagement with circumstances which at some level we chose for ourselves.

The other response is silence because, for those who know the truth of life, there is nothing really to be said. Life just is. And even if the secret could be spoken, no one would believe it, for all have to take their own journeys to arrive at the place of the Soul Warrior (and some, of course, never will).

"For those who have had the experience, no words are necessary. For those who have not, no words are possible," as the spiritual philosopher Ram Dass once wrote.[3]

As the Soul Warrior, we reside in the place of laughter and silence, where we begin to sense what it means to become the wise Elder for the communities we serve. For many traditional peoples like the Ninja, who were born into hardship and for whom survival itself was a miracle, living to old age was a sign of power, and the Elders were sought out as holders of sacred and practical knowledge. They were the *meijin* and *wanjin* (the "masters," and "men of harmonious spirit") who had made the journey of the initiate themselves and discovered answers that might serve as signposts for others.

These ancient and revered ones had magic to impart, insights into living, stories to tell, and wisdom to pass on, in a way our Western lifestyles have no place for. We shuttle our elders away into "care homes" and annexes so we never hear their stories, and we all live half-empty lives as a consequence. We continually have to reinvent the wheel and find our place again because we have lost the guidance of people who have lived the story of our lives and walked the path we are on.

Our elders feel devalued; their life mission and all they have discovered becomes a joke to be tolerated, and they are left to question themselves, so their vision becomes weak. In such circumstances, we are children without parents, people with no model to aspire to.

In less chronological terms, an Elder-to-be—or Soul Warrior—is anyone who has made the journey through the gates of fear, power, and confusion, and has now engaged with the final enemy: soul fatigue. Soul fatigue is an experience we are perhaps all familiar with: a sense of grief, suffering, ennui, or boredom with the world—that "is it all worth it" feeling that, no matter what we do, we can change very little and must accept our lot as stoically as we can. It is the time, Castaneda tells us, when a person has an "unyielding desire to rest . . . [but] if he gives in totally to his desire to lie down and forget, if he soothes himself in tiredness, he will have lost his last round. . . . His desire to retreat will overrule all his clarity, his power, and his knowledge. But if the man sloughs off his tiredness, and lives his fate through, he can then be called a man of knowledge."[4]

Most commonly, the feeling of soul fatigue comes with endings: the end of a relationship, for example, when, after all the struggles to connect, all the promises made and the love given, we realize that we haven't come far enough for a real breakthrough and here we are again, facing the journey to love all over again.

It is easy to give in to the temptation to withdraw from life or give up on love at such times, but if we hold on to the understanding that every ending is also a new beginning, and accept that with our pain comes growth, we can focus instead on the gifts we have received.

The shadow of the Soul Warrior—one who cannot meet this challenge and has embraced his "desire to rest"—is the "Poor-me" or Cynic, the person who is out of passion for life, who has given up and wants you to do the same. He or she is the person who laughs at your desire for spiritual development, the work colleague who tells you, "You'll never get on in this place," the rejected lover who warns you not to get too close to others because "no man/woman can be trusted."

The strategy of the Cynic is to escape from life in these ways, so she does not have to feel her pain or risk more of it, and to take you with her to bolster her worldview and gain comfort from your company. The best strategy for the Soul Warrior wrestling with the power of the Cynic is to ground herself with real and practical projects so she does not become lost in a head-based fantasy of a cruel and capricious world. Because every one of us will create our world through our beliefs and actions in it.

This direction of the spiral is represented by the Godai element of Earth (chi), symbolizing the need for grounding and readiness to apply the learning of the journey to the task of living in the real world. When the Soul Warrior touches the Earth in this way, she also touches the Void which, for the Ninja, is "the 'nothing' from which all things take their form . . . the emptiness of potential, the source of all that is [which] gives rise to creative capability and the ability to direct the body's energies."[5] The Soul Warrior then becomes the Mystic.

The Mystic

The only devils in the world are those running around in our own hearts. That is where the battle must be fought.

—MAHATMA GANDHI

Element:	Void
Experienced through:	All human qualities (physical, emotional, mental, spiritual)
Exploration of the world through:	Oneness
Aim of the Mystic:	Harmony and flow
The Mystic's gift:	Completion
Ninja principle used to reveal this gift:	*Wa* (harmony of being) and *heiho* (warrior strategy)
Gateway:	None
Shadow:	None
Manifestation of the shadow:	None
Chronological age:	None
Stage of the journey:	Arrival—the Elder

The Mystic has integrated all the archetypal energies within the psyche and can draw upon them with intention and focus instead of falling prey to their shadows. For this reason he or she stands at the center of the spiral, as we see in our archetypal map.

But he also takes himself lightly, recognizing that his foibles and weaknesses are a part of who he is and he is no different from anyone else, not a god or a guru, merely human. "Upon the highest throne in the world, we are seated still upon our arses," as the philosopher Montaigne put it. The greatest achievement of the Mystic, therefore, is that he has simply learned to accept himself in all his richness and allowed this to become his single strategy for living.

The Mystic is in many ways similar to the divine fool of the tarot, the person who is untouched by disaster or negativity, no matter what life throws at him. He is one with the Tao, in control of his power, and able to flow with life itself. He has made the circuit of the Four Gates and is, in many ways, the Lover once again, in touch with the pure consciousness we all had when we were first born into this world. Because of this, he willingly takes on the role of Elder, becoming an example to others by his actions in the world.

The step of the Soul Warrior into the Void and the Elder role is an automatic one. There is no initiatory challenge to pass, merely quiet acceptance of who we are, for once we traverse the complete circuit, we understand the nature of the world and can live our lives with all the freedom and happiness we decide to allow ourselves.

Making the Journey, Approaching the Gates

Perhaps you feel the presence of these archetypes within you? Good. Then you have the potential to complete the journey. Don't underestimate this: 99 percent of people never even question their realities or look beneath their surfaces. You are already a member of the warrior elite.

Next, however, you must integrate these energies if you are to consider yourself fully initiated into conscious living. The chapters that follow offer you techniques for doing so. Here, though, is a brief introduction to the gateways you will walk through and what they might mean for you.

Fear—The Gateway to the Lover

Fear represents our inability to move forward as a result of our assumed or accepted fears or our unwillingness to face the challenges ahead (a situation the Ninja knew as *kyoha*). Fear can also be beneficial, however, because it provides a breakthrough moment, a coming alive to the understanding that we are facing the unknown instead of relying on habits, received wisdom, or secondhand information to build a picture of ourselves and the world. It means we have at least woken up and taken our first steps on the path with heart. Of course, if we allow our fears to get the better of us, then rather than follow that path we may crumble, fall back into routines, and never get to experience an authentic life with all its rewards. The option to crumble is always the easiest, because then we will never have to look at who we are, what the world is. The downside is that we will never know ourselves or get anywhere worth the going, either.

Power—The Gateway to the Seeker

Issues with power arise when we become stuck in old patterns, particularly on an emotional level (what the Ninja called *kisha*—the trap of self-indulgence or self-importance). Power can trick us into believing that we know ourselves (that we are rich and successful magnates, for example, when we are really defining ourselves in terms of a role). It may also suggest to us that, having faced our fears, we can now rest in the full knowledge of who we are and all we are truly worth (which is actually a very limiting proposition).

Confusion—The Gateway to the Magus

Confusion is the inability to use our minds skillfully for self-reflection and the pursuit of personal truth. When we live in confusion, we get lost in unworkable outcomes and are unable to find a vision and purpose for ourselves that has clarity and strategy to it.

Soul Fatigue—The Gateway to the Soul Warrior

To the Ninja, this willingness or desire to give up at the last minute as a result of tiredness or boredom with the process was known as *rakusha*—"laziness" or "temptation." It is that feeling of asking ourselves, "Is it *really* worth it? Will I ever know myself or get what I want? Is there no end to this?" and responding without courage, so we renege on our commitment to see things through.

But there is also another form of soul fatigue that stands as the final trickster between the Soul Warrior and the entrance to the Void. This trickster masquerades as enlightenment but is actually a manifestation of powerlessness, or "softheartedness"—the inability to use our powers effectively. This might occur for any number of reasons, but a frequent one is that, in our new "enlightened" state we feel such a connection with all things that we lose sight of ourselves and no longer take responsibility for our actions or the achievement of our objectives.

This error, known as *ashia* to the Ninja, is illustrated by a man I once knew, a Buddhist, who saw himself as highly enlightened and felt so much compassion for all living things that he almost killed himself through personal neglect. At first, he would not eat meat because he could not hurt another living being. Then his concern spread to the suffering he perceived in vegetables and fruits, until finally he would eat nothing and, indeed, preferred to walk five miles out of his way rather than cross a park for fear of hurting the grass.

Behaviors like this are taking responsibility for everything *but* oneself. They are the obsessions of a highly *un*enlightened person, as they are also a fall back into fear (in this case, fear of leaving a mark on the world, or in other words, fear of living), which is the very first of our initiatory challenges. This man only survived at all because someone else took responsibility for him and ensured that he was helped.

We will explore these gateways in more detail in the chapters that follow, as we learn ways to pass through them using the power of our own resources.

FACING THE FEAR, WALKING ON FIRE

Success is not the result of spontaneous combustion. You must set yourself on fire.

—REGGIE LEACH

There are twenty feet of hot coals in front of me, some of them still flaming. On this firewalk the temperature underfoot will be 1200 degrees. I want to do this because I want to know what I'm capable of—in my mind and my body. Can a human being really walk on hot coals and remain unburned? The Shugendo Ninja mystics knew the answer to this. They would train themselves to walk through fire to prove their mastery of the elements, as well as of their own fears. And so here I stand before this path of flame, watching as two others make their journey across the embers, laughing as they walk. They don't look harmed, but then, they've done this before so they know the technique—if there is a technique.

I look at the coals a while longer. And then I become aware of this almost-fog in front of me, like a barrier of mist. I know it is a wall of my own fear—something I've created for myself—and there's actually nothing there at all, no mist, no almost-fog, but the image for a moment is compelling. Then I laugh at myself and step onto the fire.

Twelve hundred degrees, yet nothing hurts. I stand there a while, then walk to the end. Still nothing hurts. Later I'll walk it again—ten times in all, sometimes dancing on the coals—and at the end of it I will reflect on this simple fact: that I felt more pain in my imagination while standing at the entrance to the firewalk, staring into the mists of fear, than I did when I set foot on the path. The fire itself was pain free. It is our illusions that hurt.

Three

ka (fire): The Lover meets fear

The Origins of Anxiety

Humans fear everything. They have spent eons learning how to be afraid. Now they must learn how not to be afraid. . . . Because they will not gain their balance as long as they are gestating fear . . . man's fear is surpassing man's experience of his passion for living. . . . [Fear] has become their dominant motivator, and it is their biggest obstacle.

—Chea Hetaka

As a modern society, we have thrown ourselves head first from the high cliffs of sanity into the sacrificial flames of fear. Its fire laps around us everywhere—in our newspapers, on television, in our bureaucracies, in the work-plane-car rages we see in our offices, skies, and streets, in the warnings of parents to their children. With it come the cohorts of fear: blame, guilt, overprotection, the revenge and recrimination of gang warfare, marital disputes, drive-by shootings, explosions of violence, and the "terrorism" and territorial wars that break out across the globe with the same old ferocious monotony.

It begins subtly, this fear, with a mood of the world, an ingrained and unquestioned belief about the way things are, a narrowing of focus from a vast space filled with stars and potential to a half-lit cul-de-sac of dramas and disappointments. Finally, fear becomes so institutionalized—in our newspapers, in the mythology we accept as fact in our schools (every history lesson the story of a war, every geography class the landscape of a divided world)—that we become habituated to it and are no longer aware of an alternative. It is there as background noise, a subtle and unconscious influence that saps our energy and holds us back from the very things that made life attractive to us when we were first born and experienced our Lover energy. Fear is not natural; *we learn to be afraid.*

A few nights ago, for example, I switched on the TV and sampled the various channels to see what choices I had. On the first channel, I could watch a documentary about air traffic controllers, which taught me that human error and mechanical failures are increasing in our skyways—so now I know that my instinct for adventure, excitement, and travel is not to be trusted, for they are dangerous things, these blue open skies of ours.

On the next channel I could watch another documentary, one which told me that football hooliganism is now at an all-time high—so enjoying my leisure with a football match or a walk past the grounds is no longer a safe pursuit.

Better leave the city for the country then. But even that isn't safe, according to the commercials on channel three—not unless I can ensure my survival on our "lethal roads" by buying a car with side impact protection.

And when I get to the countryside? No fun (or security) there either, according to the drama on channel four, about murder in a small rural village, where gun-toting maniacs lurk behind every tree.

Channel five? No better. The program there was about surveillance cameras and how they are "aiding the fight against crime." The tiny frightened island of Britain now has more CCTV cameras than any other country on Earth, including the United States. We need them to help ward off (or at least record) the threats that await us on every street corner, it seems. Yet, despite having so many of these devices (in excess of four million) that they would fill hundreds of junkyards many times over, the police tell us we need still more because our country is such a dangerous place.

If I listened seriously to these televised words of doom that define my world as fear filled and hostile, I would be too terrified to ever venture out again. I'd sit at home instead and worry about just how many more safety locks I need on my doors.

Yet if I reflect on my life for a moment, it becomes self-evident just how much crap I have allowed into my home from programs such as these. How many plane crashes do I really know about? Maybe half a dozen, if that, in the whole of my life and a hundred safe plane trips of my own. How much football hooliganism have I experienced? None, and I have lived next to two football fields. How many car crashes or murderers behind trees have I had to deal with? Murderers: zero. Car crashes: one—and that was my own fault.

Television producers will always choose bad news over good and fear over joy because that's what wins the ratings wars. But consider this: in 2003, for example, the murder rate in the United States went *down* by 20 percent. In the same year, news coverage of murders went *up—by 600 percent.* The truth is that the very scarcity of disaster is what gives producers their drama since statistically we live in a safer world year-on-year. So why does fear win the ratings war? Because it has become our habit.

The Ninja spoke of a flow of consciousness throughout the world, the thoughts and feelings of every human being blowing like an invisible wind across the planet, creating a pool of shared awareness, a "mood of the world." Jung saw it as the collective unconscious of everyone alive. To the Ninja, it is *aiki*—the inner spirit informed by the outer world. It is the zeitgeist, the spirit of the age, our unstated assumptions and taken-for-granted knowledge of the world. It is the reality we create by projecting our beliefs outward so that these take shape and form what is or comes into being.

If we go along with the received wisdom of the present age and our dreams of fear, the world itself becomes a dreadful place, limited and limiting, frightening and unsafe. We create what we imagine to be real. These flames of anxiety that we feed so willingly are created by our agreement to accept the dream of fear, to comply with it, and to use it to define ourselves and others—even if we are not consciously aware that we are doing so. In this way, we slip into the habit of threats and insecurities, because these are what we know.

Of course we must laugh at the pettiness behind such fear-fueled television dramas. But there is cause for sadness here too. The Lover is a beautiful, free, creative spirit, and we see so much creativity, talent, and passion in television programs like the ones I've mentioned; yet much of the passion gets lost to fear while the creativity turns into self-perpetuating shadows. The shadow of the Lover is the Wounded Lover, fearful of life, curled fetally into a ball and surrounded by a hard shell to prevent new hurts getting in. Better to be afraid and protected than wounded again.

If we—each TV producer, director, actor, or viewer—cannot meet our fears and come to understand them, defuse them, and pass through them, we have no chance of mastering Lover energy and creating real beauty, and even less of moving through this gateway to become Seekers who find the meaning in our lives.

Why is it that we have created such a world of fear? Where do these fears come from?

The Origin of Fear

The Ninja knew that our fears stem from childhood and are usually based in fantasy rather than fact, which is why they began the training of their kusa—their "little weeds"—from such an early age. Indeed, our fears often have little to do with us at all, from the point of view of our unique and personal experiences, for when we are small we have such little knowledge of the world. Instead, we absorb fear *before we are even born*. And by the time we are able to question what we have learned, we are so used to living in a world of fear that we no longer even see it as questionable.

Before we go any further, I want to offer you an exercise that explores these origins of fear in depth, so you can gain some insight into your own life and where your fears and other beliefs have come from. This is a long meditation, so I have included a number of break points throughout it. Use these as opportunities to record your thoughts, reflections, and recollections and, if you wish, leave a little time—an hour or a day—before going on to the next part, so your insights and energies can settle.

To begin with, lie down comfortably and empty your mind of conscious thought. Close your eyes and breathe for a few minutes, with deep, slow, even breaths. This is *kokyu chikara*—the use of the breath to find stillness. When you are ready, take a look at the first section of statements and the questions that follow. Then close your eyes again and allow yourself to "dream" the scenario described and find answers to the questions asked. Don't think it through, simply note the images that come to mind and the feelings and sensations in your body, and be aware of your inner knowing. After a break, repeat the process for the next section.*

EXERCISE 1
Shibou: *The Conception Journey*

First of all, allow yourself to merge with the consciousness of your father before the time when you were conceived. "Become" your father, the person he was before you knew him, and experience his life as he did. As you do so, ask yourself:

---

*This meditation is based on an exercise developed in large part by Howard G. Charing and taught by Howard and myself in the "Four Gates to Freedom" and "Path of the Hero" workshops we run together. Howard has a Web site at www.shamanism.co.uk.

Why might I choose this man as my father?
What lessons might I learn from him?
What has his life been like?
What are his hopes, fears, ambitions, regrets?
How does he live his life as a man?

Now see your mother at a time before you knew her and allow yourself to merge with the consciousness of this woman before you were conceived. Ask yourself:

Why might I choose her as a mother?
What lessons might I learn from her?
What has her life been like?
What are her hopes, fears, ambitions, regrets?
How does she live her life as a woman?

Do any of these feelings, hopes, fears, regrets, seem in any way familiar to the ones you know in your own life now?

Now see your mother and father together, interacting with each other, at a time before you were conceived.

How does your father feel about your mother?
How does she feel about him?

Are these feelings familiar in relationship patterns of your own?

Record your observations.

Some time has passed and your parents have made a decision (consciously or not) to have a child together—you. We join them at the moment of their lovemaking, which will lead to the conception of this child.

Allow yourself to merge with the consciousness of your father's sperm as it is released and begins to describe the journey, the story, of your life. Millions of sperm are released, millions of potential you's,* but only one will be successful.

What is the consciousness—the feelings, the hopes, the fears of this one successful sperm, and of those that fail?

What might a possible other you have been like?

Now let yourself merge with the consciousness of your mother's egg.

What are its feelings, hopes, fears?

The egg for the first time sees the sperm it knows will fertilize it.

What are its feelings—toward itself and toward the sperm it sees?

The sperm also sees the egg for the first time and knows it will be successful, that it will meet with and fertilize this egg.

What are its feelings—toward itself, toward the egg, and toward the sperm it knows have failed?

Are any of these feelings in any way familiar to you?

The egg and sperm come together in the moment of conception and a new consciousness is created—you. From the perspective of this consciousness:

What is this meeting like?

Does it feel deliberate or unplanned?

Does the egg suck the sperm in, or is it the sperm that makes directly for the egg?

How do the egg and the sperm both feel at this meeting of their individual consciousnesses?

---

*The miracle of you: More than 69,949,000,000,000 different chromosome combinations can result from fertilization. That's almost seventy thousand billion other "you's" that could have existed. When you consider that this is from one successful sperm (which could equally as well have been unsuccessful), you begin to realize what a miracle you are—so easily, *you* might not have been born at all. Something else to ponder: if you imagine six generations of your family standing behind you, that amounts to 1,000,000 people. If any *one* of these people wasn't there, you might well have not existed.

The sperm is aware that conception will result and that it will now somehow die to all that it was.

What are its feelings at this paradoxical moment of life and death—
toward you, itself, the egg that it is now a part of?

The egg is also aware that conception will result and it, too, will die, as a new consciousness (you—the growing child) takes over.

What are its feelings toward you, itself, the sperm that is now a part
of it?

Are these feelings in any way familiar to you in your life now?

The tiny new life that is created by this union—you—is aware of itself and all of the moods and feelings that surround it. From this perspective:

What are your feelings at this moment of conception?
What do you already know about yourself?
About those around you?
This body you are a part of?
This world you are a member of?

Are these feelings in any way familiar in relationship patterns of
your own?

Record your observations.

We have moved on in time once more and your mother is aware that she is pregnant.

What are her feelings about this discovery?

Your father is told.

What are his feelings?
What is your mother's reaction to your father's feelings?
What is your father's reaction to your mother's feelings?

As a conscious life with feelings of your own, you are aware of all of these reactions.

What are your feelings about the emotions and reactions your parents have toward you—and toward each other (has anything changed)?

What feelings do you have toward your parents and yourself?

Are these feelings in any way familiar to you now or in relationship patterns of your own?

Record your observations.

During your mother's pregnancy there may have been a problem, a drama, or a trauma of some kind—or more than one. From the consciousness of the growing fetus:

Was this the case for your mother and/or for you?

What were your mother's feelings about the pregnancy and toward you before this problem?

What are her feelings, hopes, and fears now this problem has taken place?

What were your father's feelings about the pregnancy and toward you before this problem?

What are his feelings, hopes, and fears about the pregnancy and toward you now?

Are these feelings in any way familiar to you during problem situations in your life?

What judgments did your mother make about herself as a consequence of this problem?

What judgments did your father make of himself?

What judgments did they make about each other and about you?

Are judgments (or self-judgments) like these in any way familiar to you when problems arise in your own life?

In what situations or circumstances do you experience these feelings and judgments? Who in your life makes you feel these things?

This problem—whatever it was—was resolved in some way.

How was your problem resolved?

How did your mother and father feel about this resolution?

What agreements did they make with each other, with you, or with some higher power in order to resolve this problem?

Are these feelings or agreements in any way familiar to you in your own life or relationships?

Record your observations.

We move ahead in time again, to your mother's first contraction.

What are her thoughts and feelings at this time?

What does she do?

What are the thoughts and feelings of your father?

What does he do?

What are you feeling as you sense this first contraction?

What do you do?

What judgments does your mother make of herself . . . your father . . . you . . . as her contractions begin?

What judgments does your father make of himself . . . your mother . . . you?

Do these reactions and judgments to the sudden, unexpected, or unknown, seem in any way familiar in your own life now?

Record your observations.

The child—you—is conscious and aware during the birthing process. From the perspective of this awareness:

What are the reactions and feelings of your mother during this process?

What are the reactions and feelings of your father?

What are your feelings?

Do these reactions and feelings seem in any way familiar in your life now (when you are facing pressures or constraints, for example)?

You are born and take your first breath.

How does it feel to you?

Breathe in and experience it again now.

What information or judgments about the world are carried in on this first breath?

Are these in any way familiar to you in your life now?

You look around, conscious, and aware of your new surroundings.

How does the world look?

How does it feel?

You see your mother and father for the first time.

What are your feelings toward them?

How do you react?

How do they react to you and what do they feel about you?

What are their first words to you?

What is your first thought—about this world you have been born to, about your mother, your father?

How do you react to their words?

Do these feelings and thoughts seem in any way familiar to you in your life now (when meeting new people or entering strange situations, for example)?

Record your observations.

The cord is cut that ties you to your mother. For the first time in your life you are an independent being, still reliant on others, but able to operate with some autonomy and express yourself to make your own needs known.

What is your first feeling in response to this?

Your first thought?

Your first action?

Your first need?

Do these feelings, thoughts, actions, needs, seem familiar in your life now (when you are faced with circumstances of freedom or choice, for example)?

Were your first needs met?

By whom, and when?

What conscious or unconscious judgments did you make about yourself/your parents/the world around you as a consequence of having your needs met/unmet?

Is this meeting (or not) of your needs in any way familiar in relationship patterns of your own?

Are the (self-)judgments you made all those years ago still familiar to you now when your needs are met/unmet?

Record your observations.

The newborn—you—is given food (nourishment) for the first time. From your perspective as a conscious newborn:

Is this in reaction to your request, or to your mother's desire to feed you?

What are your thoughts, feelings, reactions, to this first feeding and toward your mother as a consequence of being fed?

What are your thoughts, feelings, reactions, toward your father?

Are these sensations in any way familiar in your life now when you are nourished or nurtured by another?

We all make (unconscious) contracts with our parents and sometimes these may even seem contradictory. For example, toward mother, "If I am sweet and do not cry, you will love and take care of me," or toward father, "If I cry loudly to get my needs met, you will love and take care of me."

What was your contract with your mother and father?

What was their contract with you?

From the perspective of a growing child, do you feel that these contracts were honored? By you? Your mother? Your father?

Are these contracts in any way similar to those you make in relationships now?

Are there any similarities between the way these first contracts were honored (or not) and the outcomes of the relationship contracts you now make?

Record your observations.

We move on again in time, to the adult who is making this meditation, but still connected to these early energies. From the perspective of one who has made this epic journey from conception to birth, with all the learning that has taken place:

What do you understand as the overriding feeling or mood of your life?

What do you believe your life to be about?

What do you now sense about your relationships with:

Fear?

Power?

Freedom?

Happiness?

And love?

Record your observations.

Now close this book. Do not return to it for nine days.

The Womb as a Cradle of Fear

You were asked to leave this book for nine days. Did you? Or did you carry on reading? Whichever choice you made tells you something about your relationship to fear, authority, and personal power. It may be useful for you to meditate on this: "Why did I leave this book because I was told to?" Or, "Why did I continue to read when I was asked to put it down?" There is no judgment here, no right or wrong response, nothing you should or should not have done; it is simply something to reflect on.

The reason I asked you to give it nine days, by the way, is simply that, having undertaken this meditation myself, I know that it can open up a box of memories, images, and recollections, sometimes as remembered events, sometimes in dreams and symbols, and these can be as powerful as the meditation itself. The Ninja say it takes nine days for any action in the world to reveal its true effect. It is worth the time to allow our souls to lay bare these other aspects in the poetry of dreams.

This meditation is similar to one of the first exercises my sensei (Ninja master) gave me, a reflection on *shibou*. This Japanese word translates variously as "mortality," "desire," or "ambition," the implication being that our soul or spirit has a purpose when we are born but it also means, simply, "fat" or "blubber," the notion being that we may be carrying fear and other weight that is unnecessary and perhaps not our own, but coming from others (notably our parents). There is more on this later.

It may be that during this meditation or the days following it, you asked yourself, *Are the things I am sensing and feeling real, or am I imagining them?* There are two answers to this:

1. Only you know, and

2. It really doesn't matter.

Orthodox (or, perhaps, archaic) Western medical opinion tells us that we have no memories of life in the womb, or indeed, much before the age of five, because it takes that long for the memory centers of our brains to develop. More interesting research, however, suggests that our first experiences of life, our first desires and passions, as well as our first sensations of fear, come not from physical interactions with the world, but from our experience of the womb itself. How can this be if we do not yet have memory centers to store these experiences?

Simple. We have something much more useful than a brain;* we have a body—and it is through the body, its sensations and experiences, the Ninja believe, that we first use our Lover energy to explore the world. It is the body, not the brain, that remembers.

In my book, *The Journey To You*,[1] for example, I quoted the work of brain scientist Karl Pribram, who suggests that our entire body is like a hologram, every part of it storing memory. This is not so different from the Ninja concept of tai sabaki—the truth of the body. In Pribram's experiments, rats were taught to run mazes and then had the memory centers of their brains removed. Remarkably, however, they could still remember their way around the maze. Their bodies remembered.

In a similar vein, in *The Secret Life of the Unborn Child*, Drs. Thomas Verny and John Kelly write that mothers who have emotional problems can pass their fears on to the unborn children carried in their wombs. "Silence or chaos often leaves deep mental scars on the youngsters. At birth they tend to have far more physical and emotional problems."[2] Once again, the body—from a time before the brain is well developed— remembers the experience of the womb.

---

*Indeed, as remarkable as it seems, we can exist quite happily without one. When a Ph.D. student was referred to him by a colleague at Sheffield University, Professor John Lorber examined the student and found he had an IQ of 126 (which is pretty good); he also had a first-class mathematics degree. In his intellectual and physical appearance the student was first rate. But a brain scan revealed a different picture: *he had no brain*. His cranium was filled with cerebrospinal fluid and his cortex was just a millimeter thick (a normal thickness is 4.5 centimeters). Cases like this, of successful people who have little or no brain, are rare but not unheard of. In fact, quite a few people may go through life happy and healthy with very little brain matter at all. Maybe the condition is less rare than we think. Since testing for brain disorders is so infrequent, how would we even know *who* has *what* amount of brain, unless some other anomaly occurred? The point is: if people can get by just fine with very little brain, then where *are* memories, consciousness, and so on, actually stored? According to recent research, they are more likely to be found in the body (or the energetic field that surrounds it). For more information on brain research, go to www.bbc.co.uk/health. For more information on this particular field of inquiry, see my book *The Journey To You* (Bantam, 2001).

Verny and Kelly report on the findings of Dr. Stirnimann, a Swiss pediatrician, who carried out research along similar lines. Studying the sleeping habits of newborn children, he found that the child's sleep patterns were also set in utero and reflect exactly the mother's own habits. The life of the child was influenced by its prebirth experience.[3]

In their more poetic book, *Conscious Conception,* Jeannine and Frederick Baker write about their research over a number of years during the conception, gestation, birthing, and rearing of their six children. One of their conclusions is that "the flow of life-force is contained by our conscious conceptions. . . . As we contained our babies in utero, we continue to hold the behavioral field of our children."[4]

These studies all show a link between mother, father, and child at all stages of the pregnancy, from the point of conception onwards—all of which is actually quite obvious if you think about it. This link was well known to warriors of all traditions. The Bon shamans, for example, understand that we are already one year old when we are born and that "Before our first breath, we have been conditioned by our psychosomatic experiences in the womb. . . . We come into each physical life with certain qualities and habits already influencing our behavior."[5]

Despite all this research and opinion, however, only you know the answer to the question "Was what I experienced in this meditation 'real'; did it really happen as I saw it?" Only you can feel the truth of it in your body, your gut reaction to the information you received.

This leads us to the second question, and the answer: it doesn't actually matter if the events you saw "really" happened just as you experienced them in your shibou meditation. Because whatever you believe to be true you will make real anyway. Our entire lives are, in this sense, an act of faith; whatever we place our belief in determines the results we get. This is what the Ninja meant when they spoke of the mythic quality of human life and the need to free ourselves from our beliefs and limitations. If I believe I will be burned by hot coals, for example, I may hesitate and act with indecision and so get burned. If I believe the coals won't harm me, I stride forward with purpose and remain unharmed. Similarly, if you believe that the experiences of your conception journey were as this meditation showed them, then they are real—because you are living your life as if they were, in any case.

Having said that, there do tend to be remarkable correspondences between what we sense instinctively to be true and what did truly happen. One man, having worked through this meditation, decided to speak with his mother about it. Here is his story:

In my meditation I saw myself lying in the mud at the bottom of a pit next to a fetus. I knew that it was dead and it was me. I looked up and I saw my mother having an abortion. I was even aware of the date (late 1948). I was shocked to see my father complicit in this, and wondered how he could do it, knowing his strong religious background and his views on family.

The vision moved forward to a second pregnancy and then to my birth and I witnessed my mother in labor on the delivery bed. All my senses were active. I could smell the fresh paint on the walls of the operating theater and watched the surgeon perform a caesarean operation. Listening to him, I knew there was an expectation that I was dead, as there was no sign of life.

I saw the surgeon lift me up, but then the baby—I—started to move. I heard the first words of my life—those of the shocked surgeon: "It's alive!"

Some time later I discussed this with my mother. After her initial surprise it was clear that she needed to get this off her chest and she was very frank and open about it. She confirmed that she did have an abortion in 1948. She also confirmed how she did it (which was as I'd seen it), and my father's role in this.

She then confessed that she tried again in 1949 when she had become pregnant for a second time (that would have been the "me" that made it). She was really surprised when I asked her, "Who said 'It's alive!' at my birth?" and she asked me how I knew. She then confirmed it was the surgeon who had been called in as it was an emergency to get the "dead" baby out.

This startling revelation led to a beautiful reconciliation with my mother. She told me what had happened, her motives, and about my father. This explained a lot for me because at an intuitive gut level I never trusted my mother, and now I knew why. (At an unconscious level, I knew she had tried to kill me.)

From this I also got a profound insight into "what makes me the way I am," and I understood how that remark "It's alive" had influenced my life, as my response to living has always been "I'll fucking show them I'm alive!"

I sometimes wonder at the surgeon's words, though, and at how different my life might have been if the first words I had heard were not "it," along with surprise at my existence, but "he's a beautiful baby boy," or something similar.

We know far more than we think, and we carry the fears, hopes, and life experiences of our parents within our emotional DNA. Because we believe that we cannot *really* know these things, however, we often accept the fears of others as our own. The fears you have, though, may never have been yours at all.

This is reminiscent of don Juan's words to Castaneda as he explained how and where we gain our life energy: "The Level of Energy of all beings depends on three fundamental factors: the amount of energy with which they were conceived, the manner in which the energy has been utilized since birth, and the way in which it is being used at the present time."[6]

We look further at the utilization of this energy in the next chapter.

FOUR

FEAR, FREE WILL, AND FREEDOM

Seeing Fear for What It Is

When there is a light in the darkness which comprehends the darkness, darkness no longer prevails.

—CARL JUNG

Don Juan's words about the source of our life energy, beyond the initial boost of our conception—"the manner in which energy has been utilized since birth, and the way in which it is being used at the present time"—refers to something else we know to be true: that we have been skewed by the world around us into expending our energy on fear. We are socialized by images from programs like the ones mentioned earlier, by the words of our parents, teachers, experts, and leaders. Part of our Lover energy, our passion for life, is lost to us as the institutions that serve our fearful dreams work cumulatively upon us to instill the habits of fear.

Socialization begins early. The first description we ever receive about ourselves, for example—and so natural has it become to us that we don't even question its meaning—is that of *boy* or *girl*, the label applied as soon as we are born. In a study in the 1970s, psychologists dressed newborn boys in pink and girls in blue and handed them to adult women, then watched the reactions of these grown-ups. They behaved toward the children entirely in terms of their clothing (pink or blue) and, therefore, in terms of their expectations of how boys and girls *should* behave. "Boys" (actually girls dressed in blue) were encouraged to be loud, active, and aggressive; "girls" to be quiet, receptive, and passive—based entirely on the clothes they were wearing.[1]

The significance of this simple experiment is enormous because it reveals the behavioral expectations that are applied to every child, by which he or she will learn how to live and die in the world. Boys grow up to become cannon fodder in wars, or go-getting corporate goons, by accepting a myth of themselves that they must be dominant and aggressive (whatever these terms really mean), while girls may become timid "home-makers" or even forego their freedoms by adopting the passive behavior expected of them. In this way our potential (which may be vast) becomes focused on one tiny agenda that sets our course for life at a very fundamental level. Both genders also learn to react fearfully to being seen as different than they "should" be. The "cut-throat" female executive is still looked down upon, after all, while the pacifist or "overly feminine" boy is ridiculed as gutless or "gay."

Such judgments are not part of the Ninja Way, nor of many traditional societies. Some cultures recognize more than seventy different sexual orientations, for example, not just the two that we accept. For the pragmatic Ninja, these sexual differences were not areas for criticism, but *skills* of the individual that could be used for spiritual advancement as well as physical survival.

In the modern West, however, our preoccupation with labels such as these can lead to confusion, not opportunities. Who are we really, beneath all these expectations and projections? What was your original face, the one you had before you were born?—as the Zen masters ask. It is difficult to know. Our minds, from the day we are born (or even before that), are in some sense no longer our own. And yet, we *must* know who we are if we are ever to live a real and fearless life.

If we do not know our own minds, our selves, our essence—and those around us do not know who they are any more than we do—then the entire world we occupy is based on fantasy, illusions, and the fear of judgment. This is not the agenda of the Lover, whose simple mission is to enjoy life and to play, without fear.

Gaining insight into how much you really know about yourself is simple enough, though sometimes quite surprising when the facts of the matter sink in. I offer students the following exercise in my workshops.

EXERCISE 2

Wagami (Myself): Descriptions of You

Below is a list of unfinished sentences, descriptions that we have all applied to ourselves (or had applied to us) at one time or another. Choose any one of them (or more if you wish) and finish the sentence, talking out loud, in front of a mirror. Pay careful attention to your body as you do so—how you feel as well as how you look—and any body language you notice. Aside from this, the only stipulation is that you continue speaking for no less than three minutes.

Whenever I am under pressure, I . . .
I only feel loved when . . .
I get angry at . . .
I like it best when people tell me I am . . .
I like to think of myself as . . .
Whenever I am hurt, I . . .
I want to live my life as someone who . . .
My finest achievement in life is . . .
Nobody ever said that I was . . .
Bad things happen to me when . . .
My greatest talent is . . .
I am no good at . . .
In terms of looks and personal appearance, I am . . .
The best thing that ever happened to me was . . .
My greatest challenge is . . .

I still find it difficult to . . .

If I could have one wish come true, it would be that . . .

How did you get on? How did you feel as you were speaking? Did you discover anything deeply meaningful about yourself?

I'd be surprised if you did. When we do this exercise in workshops, one of two responses is typical: either people run out of things to say within about a minute, or else they waffle to fill the time, repeating old phrases they have heard other people use about them over the years. It seems that we actually don't know much about ourselves, and little that we do "know" is real; much of it is fiction, a myth.

As strange as that may seem, this gives you one of your best shots at freedom. Because, if so little of you is really known, then your life is still an unwritten script, a work in progress, and you can choose to be anyone you want.

What stops us from doing so is our reliance on these hand-me-down descriptions as a shortcut to who we are. The Ninja reckoned that 80 percent of our available energy is locked into habits that stem from generational and social conditioning (our "personal history"). They became expert warriors by using their enemy's reliance on habit against them and employing the element of surprise—the other 20 percent—themselves. In this way they remained largely undefeated for almost one thousand years.

Eighty percent is a big number, I grant you, but at the very least that still gives us the remaining 20 percent as our power for free will. And if we can break out of our habits and assumptions about who we are, there is so much more we might also become.

Our First Legitimate Fear

From our discussion so far, you may be wondering about your own fear. After all, if so much of what you think of as *your* fear (no matter what that might be in your particular case) was inherited through your emotional DNA, your experience of conception, gestation, and socialization into the mood of the world, just what is fear, really? Do your own fears even exist?

The answer is yes *and* no, the paradox being that even if fear is a complete invention, it still exists because you believe it to be real and so you create and live it. And every fear, whether real or imagined, can still hold you back. That is why the warrior's first challenge, his first enemy, and the first gateway he must walk through is always fear, and why every initiation includes an element of this.

Actually, there is one primary fear and one other that stems from this. Every other anxiety, phobia, fear, or neurosis is an illusion that comes from these two.

The Ninja believed that the source of fear and suffering was our separation from the Void, a god-like state where we know ourselves to be connected to all things. Before we are born as physical beings, we are spirit, imagination, pure creativity, a notion our parents have, or, if you wish, we are energy. It is in the nature of energy to pool together, like drops of water that make up an ocean, and it is this pool of sentient energy the Ninja refer to when they talk of the Void. It is the bliss state of oneness with all that is, the Buddhist nirvana of being "like a drop of water in an ocean."

As soon as we are conceived, we begin our journey into separation from this state. At first it does not seem so bad, for when we are born and begin to live our Lover energy, we are in a unique position and one we will inhabit only once (maybe twice) in our lives: we are in balance between spirit and matter, the immaterial universe we are born from and the physical world we have come into. The Lover is still connected to the flow of what-is, the breath of the Tao, while also a part of the world. This is reflected in the egoless passion of the newborn, the being-at-one with his body, and the excitement with which the young child throws himself into life.

Almost immediately, however, the Lover is taught that he cannot remain connected to this state of bliss. He will learn as he grows that he is a separate being and that the immensity of creating a world for himself rests firmly on his shoulders. It is this very aloneness (he will later realize) that unites us all: we are separate and alone and all of us one in the same experience.

Separation, then, is our first legitimate fear, and we must understand it to be free of it.

EXERCISE 3
Meeting the First Fear

Close your eyes, and breathe deeply for a few moments, into that place between heart and solar plexus. This is the seat of the soul, the place between love and will.

And relax.

Call to mind any particular anxiety you have and visualize it as a thoughtform with a number of levels to it—as an onion with many layers of skin, or sheets of paper on a flipchart. Then begin peeling back the layers.

On each layer is written a single word, taking you deeper each time into what lies beneath your apparent, surface, fear. The first word you encounter might be *performance,* for example, representing your concerns about speaking in public; the next might be *visibility,* representing your deeper anxiety of being seen for who you are; the next might be *creativity,* a still deeper fear of building a performance and finding something to say that expresses your views as an individual . . . and so on. Keep going in this way, making a mental note of the words that are revealed as each new layer is stripped away. Later, you can come back to these words and explore the associations that each has in your life. For now, keep stripping them away until you get to the last layer of onion, the last sheet of paper on the flipchart.

What is the word at the center, the one all others stem from?

In one way or another, it will always be a word that suggests a form of separation. It might be *alone* or *isolated, unloved* or simply *me.* This is your first encounter with fear (what the Ninja knew as *osore,* a word that also translates as "horror") and the most authentic fear of all: *you stand alone in the world.*

Open your eyes, breathe out—and give yourself permission to have this fear. We all do.

So powerful and universal is this first expression of fear, in fact, that all cultures have developed mythologies that either reflect upon the pain and loss of separation or try to find ways to overcome it. The story of Gilgamesh, one of the oldest in the world, concerns a mythic journey for belonging, while the Bible is full of such examples—Adam and Eve cast out of Eden by their father, Moses abandoned to the rushes by his mother, and so on. Many of the Celtic legends have a similar theme— Gwion Bach thrown to the river by Cerridwen, for example, and his heroic quest to become reborn as Taliesin, "he of the radiant brow," the inspired poet who is welcomed and adored by his entire country.

Like Taliesin, we learn early that this mother we thought we were connected to is actually *not-us*; she can deny us food, cuddles, security— life, in fact—at will; she can tend to our needs, or not. And so it begins to dawn on us that we are no longer connected to the source of our own power. We are dependent, yet separate.

This sense of separation grows as we do; by school age it is all around us, and judgments have been added to it. We know now that we can either be *right* or *wrong, black* or *white, clever* or *stupid,* that we "will go far" or "must try harder," that we are A track or D track material—forever. Underlying all of these descriptions of who we are is separation into one category or another. The child—you—was once pure consciousness, an expression of universal energy. Now one being, one potential, has been made many through the application of labels.

At this stage, according to our spiral map of the Four Gates (chapter 2), we are still in the east, learning through the body, and our minds are unrefined, so we take in these judgments without question. We do not have the life experience or mental faculties to think otherwise, and we trust our "wise elders" to know us. As we absorb what they say, each of us will come to occupy one singular and uniquely predetermined life script, separate from all others.

We begin to realize that we are no longer a part of all things as we were when we were first born; now we are alone. It is a shock to our systems and seems a form of madness for those who remember the bliss of connection that is the Void—why do people agree to live like this, so alone and so lost? Do they not remember too? Aren't we all the same? The silence that greets our questions merely reinforces our confusion. We *know* we are one, and even our teachers, politicians, and priests tell us we are "all equal," we all have the same chances, the same rights, a share in the same love of God—and yet the evidence of our senses and our feelings of loss tell us something different.

The mind cannot live with two discordant ideas at the same time. It is impossible to balance such contradictions without falling into madness. Psychologists call it cognitive dissonance, this pain of making opposites connect, of trying to fit two pieces of a puzzle into only one hole. And so, over time, we begin to lose our hold on this one-time dream of connection and embrace the convention of separation instead.

All anxieties stem from this source. A fear of death, for example, is really an acknowledgment that you will be lost to the world and lose those you love one day; fear of crowds is a feeling that "in here" it is safe, while "out there" is terror. A fear of old age is the illusion that there is a "young age" you no longer belong to, whereas, in fact, all of life is simply flow and change, and "ages" do not exist at all.

Looked at in another way, however, this fear can be a great friend, because it helps us focus on what is really important. Knowing that we will one day die, for example, is actually the wisdom of a friend telling us to ignore our petty concerns and start living now, for now is all we have. (See chapter 10 for more on this and the warrior's approach to death.)

Next time you feel the presence of fear, remember what you once knew: that all there really is in this world is energy, one consciousness, the place you were born from, and that underlying all things there is no separation. That is one of the paradoxes of life: it is our standing alone that unites us.

Our Second Legitimate Fear

The knowledge of our separation leads to the understanding that we must all act alone and in our own interests. And yet, as soon as we do, we are often rebuked, either explicitly or implicitly, for being selfish, having a high opinion of ourselves, wanting too much, or simply for being who we are. Very often these words come from the people who are closest to us and should love us most (a confusion in itself) but who, nevertheless, want to control us in some way so we are not strong in our own right—because that would call into question the very basis of *their* lives. A friend of mine tells this story about a meeting with her mother:

Jayne is in her late thirties and was paying a visit to her mother who is elderly and lives alone. Her mother made tea and poured Jayne a cup, then offered her a slice of cake, which Jayne refused because she wasn't hungry. Immediately her mother began with "but it's your favorite and I made it especially for you. I've put so much work into this cake and on my pension I could barely even afford it. . . ." And so on, and so forth.

Eventually Jayne felt so guilty that she took a slice of cake simply to please her mother. As quick as a flash her mother responded with, "Hah! I thought you were on a diet! What about your figure!"

Such incidents may be nothing in themselves, but after a lifetime of this we come to understand a very simple truth about ourselves. In the words of Dr. Arthur Janov, the originator of Primal Therapy, "it all adds up to: I am not loved and have no hope of love when I am really myself."[2] And so, if he or she is not careful, the Lover, keen to please and engage with the world, becomes the Wounded Lover who is betrayed by life.

Eventually, however, the warrior must realize that giving herself away like this cannot remain an option if she wants to retain the vibrancy of Lover energy and not slip into her shadow self. She must defy her fear of mother's words, of punishment or disapproval, and find her own way. Just as Jayne eventually did, we must all refuse our mother's slice of cake.

Personal responsibility, then, is our second legitimate encounter with fear. For once we realize that we are alone in the world, every action we take becomes an expression of who we are.

This can seem daunting, since everything we then do must be a statement of intent, and every choice we make must be conscious. And yet, it is not such a big thing. Everything we do, after all, is already an expression of ourselves, conscious or not, and every action we take is evaluated, judged, and assessed as if it came from free will and independent thought. We are what we do. Whether we are awake or asleep, motivated by a willingness to take responsibility or not, we are still acting in the world, and our actions define our lives.

Fear Is Just a Description

As the Ninja know, a fear unchallenged is a description of ourselves that is handed to us by another and which we are prepared to accept. We "know" that we cannot sing, for example, because our mothers always told us to be quiet when we raised our voice in song—a perfectly natural expression of our Lover energy—and now we are afraid to sing anything in public, or even to speak our truth in front of others. A trivial example, perhaps, which nonetheless has wide-ranging consequences because these judgments that are made of us have power; they open energetic pathways into our spirit so that we draw similar experiences to us, like iron filings around the magnetic force of our assimilated beliefs about who we are. Having been told we cannot sing, we are hesitant when singing, we make mistakes, hit bum notes, and the people around us laugh, reinforcing our belief that we have an awful voice. So now we do not open our mouths at all. We become that reality and, with this, some experience of being human is taken from us.

These words of judgment (indeed, all words) have power. . . .

Language is not merely a device for communicating ideas about the world, but rather a tool for bringing the world into existence in the first place. Reality is not simply "experienced" or "reflected" in language, but is actually produced by language.

—TERENCE MCKENNA

. . . but they are still just words. And often, it is not the description itself, but our misinterpretation of its meaning that is the problem. Our minds confuse us, and we can so easily get lost in the gap between what is said and our emotional reaction to it. This is the time to go back to first principles—and the first principle of the Lover is to understand the world through the body, through tai sabaki—the truth of our physical selves—not through the mind or emotions.

Jenny was a client, an actress who had developed a fear of crowds and public performance, which was very debilitating given her profession. Through a combination of visualizations and a variation of the shibou meditation (chapter 3), Jenny was able to arrive at some clarity about the root of her problem. She remembered a dinner party her parents had given when she was about three, where she was presented to the guests and asked to "perform" for them. She felt anxious, unprepared, and nervous about being seen in this way, but she did the best she could and everyone seemed pleased with her.

Although she had forgotten this incident before our work together, she now sensed it was significant so we explored it further. I asked Jenny to scan her body and tell me where she felt her fear as a physical presence. In her stomach, she said. Whenever she felt afraid it was as if her stomach was in knots. Then I asked her to scan her body again and tell me where she felt the sensation of "performance anxiety," or whatever phrase she would use to describe her feelings before she went on stage. To her surprise, it was not in the same place at all. It was in her shoulders.

My suggestion to Jenny was that she was confusing fear with *excitement*—the natural, healthy anxiety she should feel before any performance. In fact, it was not fear of performing for others that concerned her but, based on her realizations about that night at the age of three when she was asked to deliver an impromptu performance, it was concern over not being prepared.

It may seem a simple difference, but to Jenny it was life changing. Once we had established what the real problem was, she was able to deal with it and make sure she was rehearsed and relaxed before performances. Her career has progressed in leaps and bounds. The "fear" that she originally had turned out to be a major ally for Jenny in helping her make this progression, by giving her the insight and then the tools she needed to ensure her success.

It was Jenny's body that gave her the key to this—not her mind or her brain—by circumventing the descriptions and the label of *fear*, and showing her straightforwardly what her problem really was. The body, in fact, is one of our greatest allies for connection to Lover energy, because the body knows things about us that the mind does not.

Tai Sabaki: The Truth of the Body

If you were to ask a successful lawyer how she felt, she might tell you that she was fine, pretty good in fact. "I have a stimulating career, I earn lots of money, I eat in the finest restaurants, live in a great apartment, and I'm still young and free; I have my whole life ahead of me." These are the words of the socialized mind, which measures happiness in terms of material success.

If you were to direct the same question to her body, you just might get quite a different response: "I am tired of defending people I know to be guilty or seeing those I know are innocent getting five years for nothing. The money I earn is no compensation for the way I feel or the long hours I work. I eat rich foods in restaurants that make me fat, and I am stuck sitting at a desk sixteen hours a day. I never get to exercise and I am growing unhealthy. My apartment is bland and what little time I spend there is unstimulating and boring. I never even have time to go out."

Kineshioroji (Japanese kinesiology) is a diagnostic tool known to the Ninja and, these days, a recognized physical science for asking the body how it feels in just such a way as this. It is based on the fact that our physical selves cannot lie and will not cover up the truth or become confused, as the mind often will.

In essence, kinesiology relies upon testing the physical strength or weakness of certain muscles when questions are put to us—revealing how we *feel* about something rather than what we *think* about it. The procedure is simple, and you can use it on yourself to explore your body's truth.

EXERCISE 4

Kineshioroji: *Exploring the Body's Truth*

Relax and get comfortable. For this exercise it doesn't matter if you are seated or standing, alone or with someone else. Hold out your dominant arm (the one you normally use for writing, etc.) in front of you and, in this arm only, maintain a dynamic tension so that your arm is firm, not overly stiff but not weak either. If you have a friend with you, ask your friend to test your normal strength by exerting pressure on your arm until he or she can push it down despite your gentle resistance. Or you can do this for yourself if you are alone.

Next, if you have a question you'd like an answer to, express this as a positive statement. For example, if you are in a relationship that you're not sure about or that causes you concern, your inner question might be, "Am I ready for this commitment?" Here, express this positively as: "I am ready to commit." Then ask your friend to push down on your arm again. If your arm is weaker this time (i.e., has less natural resistance), your body is telling you that you are not ready and that commitment to this relationship is indeed an issue for you.

You can double-check by making the opposite statement ("I am not ready to commit") and having your friend push down on your arm in the same way. This time it's the opposite effect you're looking for, so if your arm is stronger in response to this statement (i.e., your body agrees with what you're saying), your concerns about commitment may indeed be something for you to look more closely at.

You can use this test for any questions or fears you have in mind and to bring you closer to your Lover energy, which is the truth you know in your body.

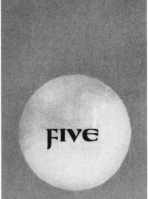

FIVE

The Initiation of the Lover: Burning Through

Techniques for Overcoming Fear

The only way to find the path is to set fire to your own life.
—RABINDRANATH TAGORE

Fear is a thoughtform, a manifestation of our personal or collective unconscious. It is passed on to us from our conception and through our socialization, the stuff of our minds. But it is the body that remembers who we are. What we require, then, to overcome fear, is a signal from the body to the mind. This is an action, a gesture, a body-to-mind communication that things are about to change.

This gesture for freedom in the face of fear is your initiation into Lover energy. With it, you reclaim what was and is already yours; you remember the simple power and passion you knew as a Void-born child.

The gestures of the Shugendo Ninja were extreme—hanging from cliffs, walking through fire, sitting beneath freezing waterfalls—but a gesture for freedom does not need to be so vast and magnificent. It could be something seemingly very ordinary. Donna, one of my workshop participants, was concerned about the environment, the loss of beauty, and the kind of world we were leaving behind for our children. For her, a gesture of freedom would be to do something about this concern. She had commitments that made drastic life changes unrealistic. So, instead of dwelling on her concern and allowing her shadow self to define the world as a depressing and dangerous place, and then teaching this to her children, she made a commitment to action—that on any journey she took, she would carry flower seeds and scatter them from the window of her car or train. This creative solution in the face of her concerns enabled her to take back power from her fears by doing something worthwhile for herself and others. It also sent a message of power and personal responsibility to her children, in a language they could appreciate.

The author Christopher Hansard gives another example of courageous self-determination when he talks of a well-to-do client who was nonetheless unhappy and had entered a "cold and isolated state." His client was a drug dealer who had come to the realization that his career was hurting everyone—himself and others—as it was out of balance with his spiritual ambitions. After discussing his feelings with Christopher, he decided to return his drug money to the communities he had taken it from and then turn himself in to the police. He served his time and emerged to start a successful new career running a charity to help people with drug dependencies. "He turned his karma around by taking responsibility."[1]

The word *karma* in this context probably needs clarification, as it is often misunderstood. It is frequently defined in the most complicated terms, having something to do with amassing debts to the world that must be paid off in other lifetimes or at the end of this one. The warrior's perspective is different, simpler, and a lot more obvious. Karma for the Ninja equates with the term *giri,* which means a sense of honor, duty, or decency (more on this in chapter 9). Put simply, it means that every action we take has a consequence for ourselves and for others in *this* lifetime. If we behave badly and without honor, it will rebound on us directly and we will end up friendless and alone. If we behave well, we will be loved in return for who we are and our lives will be happy in themselves, without the need for us to rely on the judgment and forgiveness of God or some other higher power.

Karma—or giri—is about taking back our personal responsibility.

The more conscious we make our decisions and actions, the less possibility there is of "negative karma" or, more simply, the less chance of having to sort out the consequences of our unskillful or unconscious behavior, or to rely on others to do so.

Whenever we take a conscious action—whatever it may be and in whatever way makes sense to us—we grab back our freedom and enhance our power because we also make a refusal to be bound by limitations and fears. We train the muscles of our heart to act differently by accepting responsibility for our actions. Then we can come to understand that it is not fear, after all, that we have been afraid of, but the dawning awareness of our own authority and power.

"We think that brave people have no fear," writes the Eastern philosopher, Pema Chodron. "The truth is that they are intimate with fear. . . . The trick is to keep exploring and not bail out, even when we find that something is not what we thought. That's what we're going to discover again and again and again. Nothing is as we thought."[2]

Time for Action

Identifying fictitious fears—the fears that are, deep down, not ours but the words of others that we have accepted as ours—is liberating in itself. But this knowledge is only half of the equation. *Doing something about it* is what really counts.

An accepted reality for many people is to believe that their problems were caused by (and are therefore the responsibility of) someone or something else: a lover who has hurt us, the pressures of work, the demands of living, the political system, or whatever else our excuse to ourselves may be. The fact, though, is that few of our problems were genuinely caused by others, since we are the ones interpreting them as problems rather than, for example, opportunities to shine—but even if they were the result of someone else's actions, they are still *our* problems. As warriors, we must deal with what is in front of us and deal with it ourselves. Even if someone else could provide an answer and sweep our problems away, we would still not draw authentic power from it—we would merely have found a savior and given our power to them instead. And we would always know that "our" solutions were not due to our own efforts. Furthermore, by relying on others to do the work for us, we would have learned nothing of ourselves or developed the strategies to deal with future challenges. As difficult as it may sometimes be, the only way to find ourselves and embrace our power is to take action for ourselves. As the author Ram Dass put it: "What we do in the world—our dharma—*is* our spiritual practice."[3]

Our next step, therefore, must be to seek out opportunities to do the very things that cause us to fear: to hang from our symbolic waterfalls or step onto our path of flame.

Why the need for this? Because *action*—self-knowledge applied—is the only thing that will help us break through the absorbed beliefs that have led us into the habit of self-limitation. By channeling our energies into the physical world—and away from the conceptual world where our fears live—we deny fear our energy and occupy a place where our predatory thoughts cannot consume us.

This realization is not just that of the Ninja but of all warrior traditions. Ram Dass continues: "In all spiritual practice, the strategy is the same: to identify the thing that frightens you and come as close to it as you can before you freak out. . . . Watch how the fear manifests in your body and guard against the desire to pull back. . . . As we become aware of the degree to which our fears are mind-states, rather than realities, we take our power back."

We break through our habits of inferiority by taking risks, running headlong into our fears, screaming if we need to, but laughing if we can. People who escape their limitations do so through a gesture of power. In the words of P. D. Ouspensky, "Either some unusual stimulus fills them with emotional excitement, or some unusual idea of necessity induces them to make an extra effort of will. . . . Efforts, in a word, are what carry them over the dam."[4]

Pema Chodron, in her book, *When Things Fall Apart,* writes of a man who wanted to overcome his fear but felt unable to do so. His meditation practice (mind stuff) was getting him nowhere. Finally, his teacher sent him to a small cabin in the wilderness to spend the night alone in the darkness.

Around midnight he heard a noise and, looking up, saw a huge king cobra right in front of him. The man went rigid with fear and spent the whole night staring at the snake. Finally, just before dawn, he began to cry—not out of fear though, but out of tenderness. By sitting with his fear instead of running from it, he realized that he and the snake were fundamentally the same, both alone and in darkness, and his heart was opened by this. "He felt the longing of all animals and people in the world; he knew their alienation and their struggle." He felt so much gratitude for this realization that he walked over to the snake and bowed before it. Then he fell asleep alongside its coils. When he woke up the snake was gone.

"Intimacy with fear caused his dramas to collapse and the world around him finally got through," writes Chodron.[5] If not for his action, his effort of will, to face his fear and enter the darkness, it might never have done so. Beneath our fears there is often sadness, the exquisite melancholy of knowing that we are all of us alone and facing the unknown. This is what the Ninja also meant when they spoke of experiencing the Void: it is finding the divine beauty and courage within us, which is revealed through action, not theory.

At this stage during workshops, I usually ask participants to undertake a series of "risky" exercises themselves—falling backward from a height and running blindfold toward an abyss and trusting they will be caught are two of them. The firewalk is another. In all cases, it is the surrender of the self—the death of the ego-mind, the silencing of the monkey chatter of "what ifs"—that carries them over the dam. We all live an act of faith: that we and the world are truly the way we have been taught. Making this appointment with fear, taking this risk, is a visible commitment to a different sort of faith: that we are powerful beyond measure and we *will* act without fear—even if we are shaking in our boots as we take our first baby steps toward the abyss.

I won't be asking you, in this book, to run blindfold toward a cliff. What I propose is much more sedate . . . but possibly more challenging . . .

Warrior Training

Training for the Ninja began early in life, often as soon as the child could walk. Gentle exercises, masked as games, would be introduced to help the "little weeds" strengthen their physical and mental endurance. There were games consisting of running and swimming, or leaping over fast-growing reeds so that, over the course of a summer, the child would have started by jumping a height of a few inches but by the end of the season would be diving over reeds some feet high. Because things like this were done incrementally and presented as a game, the children would think nothing of it and would enjoy the experience; but all the time they would be learning about themselves, strengthening their bodies, facing challenges and fears and, through observing their own actions and those of others, would also come to understand the workings of the mind.

Sometimes, however, a child would reach a blockage point where his fears might get the better of him and he would feel unable to continue. Don Juan tells us that in his tradition, at such moments the mentor must be "ruthless, cunning, patient, and sweet,"[6] helping the disciple to stalk his fears like a hunter after prey. This was a strategy also known to the Ninja, and they would be equally cunning in helping their young get beyond the reach of fear.

Their technique is still taught today. Students are told to locate someone within the dojo or clan who seems, from her behavior, not to share their particular fear, and to model themselves on that person. (The second student will have her own, perhaps quite different, anxieties, of course, and will also have found someone to model herself on. In this way, all students become mentors to each other.)

The next time they go into a situation that would normally cause them anxiety, each student is told to act as if they are their mentor. This strategy begins as play-acting or role-playing of a kind but, over time, students find that they become desensitized to fear through repeated exposure to it and because they have the strength of a role model to draw on. By acting *as if* they are unafraid, they *become* unafraid.

EXERCISE 5
Your Fear Mentor

My proposal to you is this: find someone who does not share the same anxieties as you. (This can be but need not be someone you know personally; it could equally well be a movie, TV, sports, or music star, or a character from a novel or comic strip.) The next time you approach a situation of fear, act in the way that person would behave. This does not mean dressing like them, making the same gestures, or using lines from their movies. It is about assuming their thoughts and freedoms.

Willingly and deliberately find situations that would normally cause you anxiety and then enter them with the full intention to experience that anxiety, but armed with the different viewpoint and abilities of your mentor. It is as if you have his or her psychological and spiritual strengths for that time. As you expose yourself to these same circumstances again and again, gradually begin to withdraw from your mentor's image, until it is just you that enters into and experiences that situation. Learn from each experience and reward yourself for each success.

EXERCISE 6
Chambara: *Playing a Role in the Theater of the Absurd*

A qualitatively different strategy for overcoming fear, similar only in that it also uses theater as a method for self-discovery, is to choose a day when, from the moment of waking until the moment you fall asleep, you stay in character as someone who expresses your anxieties to the nth degree. Effectively, you become a walking caricature of yourself.

Make sure you emphasize every tiny reaction you have to any little thing that scares you, so that everything is blown out of all proportion. This is the theater of the absurd, where all things become a comic episode as you overplay them to the point of ridiculousness. In this grand guignol of the soul all things become ludicrous—which is what our fears often are when magnified.

To the Ninja this is known as *chambara,* "theatrical combat." In psychological terms, the theater of the absurd is known as paradoxical intention. It is a way of tricking the rational mind by asking it to focus its powers on doing the very thing it doesn't want to. A person who is unable to sleep due to insomnia, for example, might try to deliberately lie in bed and concentrate on not sleeping. Or, in sex therapy, a couple who are having problems might be asked to kiss, cuddle, massage each other, or indulge in foreplay but *under no circumstances* to have sex. The effect of this is to release people from the tension of feeling that they have to sleep or make love, and they then go right ahead and do the very thing their mind was stopping them from doing.

Although modern psychology claims this as one of its techniques, the practice is actually very old. To the Ninja, it was a form of *samin-jutsu*—the art of hypnosis or self-hypnosis, the ability to train the mind to behave in a different way. Many other traditional people have an institutional joker, a *hyenkah,* or tribal fool, who plays a similar radical role of pointing out the foibles of the tribe by acting them out humorously and to excess in just such a way as the theater of the absurd exercise. Through his "insane" behavior, the fool ensures the sanity of his tribe because the people are able to look at themselves, as if in a mirror, and then make changes so that balance is restored.

The radical comic, Bill Hicks, had the same beliefs about the power of humor:

I am a shaman, come in the guise of a comic, in order to heal perception by using stories and "jokes," and always, always, *always* the Voice of Reason. . . .

If comedy is an escape from anything, it is an escape from *illusions.* The comic, by using the Voice of Reason, *reminds* us of our True Reality, and in that moment of recognition, we laugh, and the reality of the daily grind is shown for what it really is—*unreal—a joke.*

True comedy turns circles into spirals. What before seemed a tire-some, frightening, or frustrating wall, the comic deftly and fearlessly steps through, proving the absurdity of it all.[7]

The truth is this: it is your *right* to be free and happy, not caught up in dramas and fears that hold you back, and which may not even be yours. At the very least, this exercise will help you laugh at yourself and begin to play with life again, as every Lover should.

Jumonji No Kamae: Fire Movement

Long before modern psychology came up with the concept of "anchor-ing" as a way to ground our commitments and hold on to our passion and intention, the Ninja knew of its practice. The exercise that follows is a form of tai sabaki—Ninja body artistry—that you can use each day with the intention of freeing yourself from fear and realizing your ability to do so.

EXERCISE 7
Fire Movement

This begins as a fighting posture known as *jumonji no kamae,* or Fire movement. It is an offensive stance, the essence of which is to take you forward to meet any challenge head-on, with intensity and assuredness. The intention is to destroy the enemy (fear) before it has a chance to find a foothold in your psyche.

Your hands make fists; your arms are crossed at the wrists and held directly in front of your heart. Your legs are hip-width apart, with one foot slightly in front of the other (the same arm and leg leads, either left-left or right-right), and you stand slightly sideways to your imagined adversary.

As a moving meditation, you then take your back leg forward and step through as you raise your back arm up and across your face and head in an arc. Now, open your raised fist and strike forward with your hand like a knife, straight down through the fear that confronts you. Use your powers of visualization to see it vanish as you slice right through it.

Practice this movement slowly (at the speed of a t'ai chi exercise) and with full mindfulness, and repeat on both sides of the body until you feel yourself charged with power.

Mindfulness practice reveals that what we call fear is not an insurmountable obstacle, but rather a thought—or series of thoughts—accompanied by physical sensation.

—RAM DASS

Fire movement will help you cut through the illusion.

Fire: The First Ally

In the Godai system of the elements, Lover energy corresponds to Fire, the great transformer that burns away the habits and pains of the past. It is the Lover's passion, the "fire in the belly" that gets things done.

For the Ninja, Fire—ka—was the dynamic energy of expansion, "the active direction of power and control."[8] We use this energy to burn through fear.

EXERCISE 8

The Inventory: Burning Away the Past

Begin by making a list on paper of fear-filled moments from your life, in as much detail as you can. A period of quiet reflection on these things will help you. Be aware of your senses: What was happening in that situation? How did things look? What smells and sounds do you remember? How did you feel? Be as clear as possible on this.

Looking at your list, ask yourself what begins to emerge as a common theme. How did you get into these fearful situations? By not planning ahead or having a strategy for the future? By not acting consciously or taking full responsibility for your actions? By not being real or present, perhaps? What patterns do you see in the circumstances you found yourself in or your reactions to them?

No matter what happened and who might be "to blame," what responsibility are you prepared to take for creating these patterns? What, then, does this tell you about the nature of your encounters with fear?

Whenever we give our power away to events, we lose some of the energy that creates who we are. Part of our energy gets embedded in the event itself and is lost to us. We then start to generalize, so that similar scenarios carry the same weight of fear and we give more of ourselves away.

To take back your energy, revisit one of these events in your mind's eye and breathe in the threads of your power that you still see entangled there. Then breathe out the fear you have absorbed from that event into some tangible object, such as a stone you can bury along with your connections to that event.

When you feel that this particular incident has been dealt with, rip that item from your inventory and burn it, offering it to the flames as a gesture of good riddance for something that no longer serves you. See it gone and believe, totally and completely, that it is. Commit to living differently from now on.

I release you, my beautiful and terrible fear. I release you . . .
You have devoured me, but I laid myself across the fire.
I take myself back, fear.
You are not my shadow any longer.

—JOY HARJO

EXERCISE 9

The Breath of Fire

The Breath of Fire corresponds to a Ninja technique called *kokyu chikara*—a form of breath control that stirs up our energies so we reconnect with our Lover's passion.

Stand upright and draw two short breaths into the upper part of your lungs. Then breathe out a little more slowly before taking in one long breath that fills your lungs from the bottom upward so that your belly fully distends. Breathe out slowly and begin the process again.

Keep this up for a few minutes until you are familiar with the cycle, and then take your attention inward as the breath looks after itself. Repeat to yourself: "I have all the power I need to overcome my fears. The Lover is unafraid."

Use this breathing pattern and affirmation whenever you need extra energy to face any situation of uncertainty or fear. Then let your fears go. Thank them for their messages, but dare to take a chance of moving beyond them now.

WARRIOR COMMITMENT

I Let Go of Fear and Become the Lover

I am the Lover holding Fire in my hands, and I commit, with all the passion and intensity that is in me, to be true to myself, no matter what may confront me.

I listen to the messages of fear, treat them with respect, and learn from them, but I am not bound by them.

I move forward in the world, past the limitations that others have placed on me, and I live my life with integrity, in a way that serves me fully.

I make this commitment to myself with full consciousness and as a mark of self-respect and freedom.

I have every right to be free—and I choose happiness, liberty, life, and love as my expression of that right.

I let this commitment go to the universe, allowing its energy to guide and support me, and I hope and believe that things will be this way.

SIGNED: _____

DATE: _____

BREATHING WATER

Only in quiet waters do things mirror themselves undistorted.
Only in a quiet mind is adequate perception of the world.

—HANS MARGOLIUS

My face is so cold I can't tell if I'm breathing air or water anymore. It's January and I'm at the bottom of a flooded quarry, regulator in my mouth, teacher at my side. There's about thirty feet of water between us and the surface, but if I look up I can see ice floating there.

The next part of this test is easy: All I have to do is remove my air supply and breathe water.

More accurately, I have to take the regulator out of my mouth and hold it in front of me so that air bubbles up in front of my face, then put my lips to the bubbles and sip the air. To the mind, it is the same as drowning.

Time slows down when you are about to die and a lot happens in a few seconds. In those instants before I give myself to the water, I remember a line from a movie, *The Truman Show:* "We accept the reality with which we're presented." And then I remember something my Ninja sensei told me, a story of how he'd fallen into a pool as a child one summer, and sank to the bottom, unable to swim. His parents were searching for him for half an hour before they saw him on the bottom of the pool. They were inconsolable, thinking him dead. But he had been happily playing there, under six feet of water, all that time. He was still young and no one had told him that human beings can't breathe water. "We all breathe water for the first nine months of our lives," he later said. "The body knows the truth of that; it remembers."

What I have to do, by comparison, is simple; just take out my regulator and breathe bubbles of air through water. Nothing to it. I remove the regulator, allow the bubbles to dance before me, then put my face into their stream and take a breath.

Two minutes later I am still there, alive, still numb with cold. Human beings can breathe water, it seems—if we choose to believe we can.

SIX

SUI (WATER): DREAMS OF POWER AND THE SEEKER'S QUEST

On the Nature of Power

Acting is the least mysterious of all crafts. Whenever we want something from somebody or when we want to hide something or pretend, we're acting. Most people do it all day long.

—MARLON BRANDO

Our relationship to water, like our relationship to power, must be finely balanced if we are to survive it. Human beings are 70 percent water, and we must keep our natural levels close to this. Much less and we die within days; too much, and we die within minutes. Power is the same. If we have too little or too much of it we can also die—emotionally and spiritually, if not physically.

As we continue our journey we reach the south where, as our map shows, we engage with Seeker energy, and power is the thing on our minds. If we have passed our initiation into Lover energy by walking through the gateway of fear, we are now seeking direction in our lives, exploring our motivations, and looking for purpose in how we will use our newfound strengths.

Most people in the Western world have an inauthentic relationship to what they take to be power. They do not know what real power is because they have never been taught to recognize it. This can be the Seeker's greatest problem. His intention is to find purpose, but through the lure of inauthentic power he can easily be hooked into someone else's definitions and decisions about his life and so end up purposeless and, in fact, *dis*empowered. In Ninja terms, such people become *kasuka* (weak or indistinct). To understand why power is one of the most slippery, difficult, and dangerous of our enemies, we need to look at what power actually means in our society.

The Myth of Power

For many of us, issues of power and the questions around it become predominant in our teens or twenties. It is then that we are trying to make a start in life, carve a niche for ourselves, find love and companionship, and make a break from our parents so we can stand independently in the world. All of this requires us to put our attention and intention, our focus and energy (i.e., our *personal* power) into the achievement of *social* power.

What we most need at this time is guidance, approval, and support as we go out into this strange new world. But because such approval is socially conditioned and reflected in things like dot-com salaries and Gucci suits, what we get may not be the genuine support we are seeking. What we get may even be quite at odds with what we really want, and we may strive for things without knowing why we are chasing them, some of which may even be detrimental to us, as we do not know our real needs and have no Elders to guide us.

In Western society, power is defined by, and lies almost exclusively with, aging men. Aging men run our governments, corporations, banks, religious and educational institutions, and legal systems. They should be our Elders, teaching our children to be free-thinking men and women of power. But these people lack vision and courage. They have no real power of their own and thus are unable to guide others toward power.

For people who have fallen for the Western dream, "making a mark on the world" has never been about individuality but about embedding themselves deeply into a system designed to consume their individuality and use their energy against them, so it can perpetuate itself and we can consume its products. Our "Elders" have been absorbed into this system; and so they teach our young men and women how to give up their power and become Drones too, just as they have. They have no initiation to offer into a world beyond conventions because they do not know such a world. All they can really provide is the antithesis to freedom: instruction in how to give our power away.

The Seeker who falls for these dreams of aging men will never find the sense of purpose, the meaning to life, that he is looking for. He may become a Drone himself, or the other manifestation of this shadow: the Victim/Martyr who always feels like a failure, even when surrounded by Cadillacs and country homes in the Hamptons. This is because the one thing he does not have is *authentic* power—the very thing he is seeking.

Where Is the Power?

There are huge paradoxes in our Western relationship to power, the first of which is that our most "successful" people actually have little of it. Every businessman and woman who has "made it" knows they must give up their lives to their business, working long hours away from their family, interests, and passions—away from their humanity, in fact—until they become part of the business itself, as an engine is part of a car. They begin talking in terms of warfare and conflict, the outer competitiveness of the business world eroding their humanity and reflecting the conflict and unhappiness within. There are campaigns to win, targets to achieve, damages to limit, and losses to count. Perhaps they have people working for them (the troops) and authority over many whom they supervise and support, encourage and reprimand. But they are also still a servant to their workers, making sure the wages are paid and the company runs like a "well-oiled machine." They may control the destinies of many but do not really control their own.

The further up the corporate ladder the boss climbs, the less life he has, because he is also just a cog in the wheel. Andrew Carnegie, one of the richest people on Earth, was once asked why he continued to work when he had enough money to retire many times over. "I've forgotten how to do anything else," he said.

Those who "make it" may have wealth, status, even celebrity, but they often have less freedom and genuine power than when they began, and even that they may have to give away to "subordinates" and intermediaries who shield them from reality. Those that many of us aspire to be like—rock stars, movie stars, sports heroes—have people looking after them day and night. Agents, managers, PR people, secretaries, accountants, lawyers, bodyguards: these are the people who run the lives of the rich and famous and turn them into "what the public wants," not the rock stars themselves. "Everything [is] designed to stop you growing up," said Dougie Payne, bass player with the band Travis. "There are people running around doing everything for you, so you don't mature as people until something serious happens, then you go whoa, this is real life."

Our dream of power is just that—a dream—but it is a hypnotic one. And, as Thomas Paine remarked, "a long habit of not thinking a thing wrong gives it a superficial appearance of being right."

Stepping outside of society's power-program and finding *real* purpose is one of the most important things the Seeker can do to reclaim her awareness of who she is. It is also one of the most difficult of initiatory challenges, however, because we have all been conditioned from birth to define ourselves in other people's terms and to give up our power to them. Unknowingly (or even sometimes knowingly) we live out lives that have been scripted for us, unless we redefine ourselves.

How We Live Our Scripts

The Japanese word *jubaku* means "a curse or spell." It has some similarity with what the Celts called *geis*—a sacred challenge warriors must face that compels them toward certain actions. The hero's quest—and the twists and turns of our mythological stories—arises from the warrior's struggle to find a way around his or her curse, which is often cast by a parent, spouse, or other significant person.*

In one legend, the warrior Lleu was placed under curse by his mother, Arianrhod, that he might never have a name, bear arms, or take a wife—the three initiatory rights conferred on every son by his mother (symbolizing his freedom from her) when he attained manhood. Lleu's life story—his heroic quest—therefore became one of finding a wife and freeing himself by magical means. He succeeded—by creating Blodeuwedd, the "wife of flowers"—but only for a little while. Blodeuwedd went on to betray him, so Lleu was never fully able to defeat his curse, the life story his mother had handed him.

Similarly, Oisin, son of the hero Finn mac Cumaill, found himself under curse when Niamh, the faery princess, carried him off to Tir na N-Og, the Land of Eternal Youth. After three years of enchantment, Oisin began to remember his past life and miss his father, and he told Niamh of his plan to visit his homeland. Fearful that Oisin would leave her to stay with his father, she agreed to this visit only on condition that Oisin would promise not to leave his horseback or step upon the ground. Oisin promised; but on the way, disaster struck and he fell from his horse by accident. Three hundred mortal years passed by in an instant and Oisin, now ancient and dressed in rags, was left blind and wretched, never to see his true family again.

In modern psychological terms, curses such as these are life scripts that are placed upon us by the people who have power or authority over us—typically our parents—and that take the form of their projection onto us of an archetypal myth or drama they themselves feel a resonance with. A child's own identity is taken from him in increments as his life story is written and his essence defined by another. A mother's coos to her newborn son, for example, that "You're such a little baby dreamer" become subtle instructions to the young mind in how to develop and who he must be, as his mother effectively subtracts from the sum of all

---

*GeisWork uses the geis as the basis for workshops that include exercises on conscious conception, the prebirth experience, ancestral healing, and defusing the life script. See my Web site for details: www.VodouShaman.com.

he is or might become to create the one child *she* wants. She can then live her dreams through him and justify the choices she has made. "Nothing has a stronger influence psychologically on their environment and especially on their children than the unlived life of the parent," as Jung remarked.

These scripts also provide us with a comfort zone as we engage with our life stories and the parameters for living that we were given, which we remain, unthinkingly, within. By living our *story* we become habituated to it and come to regard it as truth. We cannot see an alternative because we have never had one, and so we seek confirmation for the script itself and never challenge ourselves in life—and with this, we have already bought in to giving away our power.

Jubaku: A Case Study in Family Myths and Curses

Your past is plagiarism . . . your own soul dissipates
Your history acts as your gravity.

—Joseph Arthur

A psychological interpretation of the myth of Oisin would include themes such as love, loss, and abandonment and their effects on the psyche; the contradiction between maturity and "eternal youth," and the impact on a child of an "absent father" and a controlling mother (represented by the fearful and self-obsessed Niamh). All of these themes can be seen in the case of Eli, a modern-day parallel to this myth, and an example of how easy it can be to give away power so we live out our family curse.

Eli came from a broken home, which her father had left almost as soon as she was born. She was raised by her mother, a flamboyant woman who hid her fear behind facades, including—as Eli related it—drug use, partying, and a series of disastrous sexual encounters, as she refused to grow up and take responsibility for her daughter or give her the care and attention she needed. As insecure as Niamh, her mother tried to tie Eli to her by an oath of loyalty, so that her child became her "best pal" and protégé instead of her daughter. According to Eli, the only outcome of this was that she ended up parenting (and resenting) her mother.

Having grown up in this puerile Land of Eternal Youth, Eli wanted nothing more, she said, than a stable family of her own—but she had no idea (or experience) of what a mature adult family might look like. She had been abandoned by both her father and her mother in different ways—her father by his absence; her mother by her retreat into an unreal world—and she saw herself, in archetypal terms, as an orphan (one aspect of the Wounded Lover, or the Seeker lost). She identified so strongly with this orphan image, in fact, that from the age of fourteen on, she had frequently run away from home to "make a fresh start and find her way in the world" (a pattern that stayed with her throughout her life and relationships). Little Orphan Eli—the child setting out on a quest, like the fatherless Oisin, to regain something lost and take time out from a fantasy land.

Despite her desire for stability, Eli soon embarked on a series of unsatisfying and unstable relationships of her own, just like mom. Most of these had an S&M quality to them; Eli found it comforting to receive pain along with love because this, in a sense, was all she had ever known, and she found it difficult to disentangle the two. Even here these relationships were confused, however, since Eli could never be sure if she wanted to submit to a man or control him, not quite knowing which would bring her the most safety—giving away her power and being "all her lover wanted" so he would stay with her, or taking control so she could "make" him stay.

Inevitably, such confusion over who was in charge (Eli or her lover? Eli the adult or Eli the child?) led to problems. When an unplanned pregnancy arose she kept the baby but left the child's father (just as her father had left her). She then began a relationship with a new man, during which four more unwanted pregnancies arose in almost as many months—all of them "accidents" and all terminated without telling the father-to-be—as Eli refused to grow up and take responsibility for even her own body.

She was now with another new man and pregnant again. This time the baby was wanted, but Eli and her lover were having difficulties in their relationship. This came as no surprise to anyone, given Eli's background, and they entered therapy to try to resolve their problems for the sake of their child.

We worked together for some weeks but, sadly, a few weeks of therapy could not replace years of living a script like Eli's, and one day she simply disappeared from her lover's life, just as she had from her previous boyfriends and like her father before her.

> *I am everything you lost.*
> *You can't forgive me.*
> —AGHA SAHID ALI

Saying she wanted to "make a fresh start" (again), she moved away, taking her children with her and giving her lover no contact details. In this way, she made her lover an "abandoning father" to mirror her own and her newborn son an "orphan," just like her. Eli was back in her comfort zone. (She even made sure that her lover's name did not feature on their son's birth certificate, ensuring that their child might never know his father, just as she never had.) Eli became her own single-parent mother, lost in the Land of Eternal Youth, unwilling or unable to care for the emotional health of her children or herself and angry at life and men, so continuing the family tradition.

The names we give our children are often insights into our family curse because they are the epitome of our projections onto the tiny life in front of us. As remarkable as it seems, given the rarity of the name, Eli called her new son Oisin, after the character from the myth. She was quite ignorant as to the connotations of the story, of course, thinking of Oisin as a "poet" and not an orphan, but in terms of the life script she was living and had created for her son, Eli named him perfectly.

What happens to children in these situations? Classically there are two responses. They either become bound to mother (no doubt Eli's intention) and fearful of the world outside, or they reject the mother wholeheartedly when they are old enough to ask questions and realize that they have been betrayed and prevented from living their own lives and making their own choices.

"'Bound and weary, I thought best to sulk upon my mother's breast,'" writes Robert Bly, quoting Blake, on the first of these options. "The infant boy struggles . . . fighting the narcissistic mother's desire to change him to what she wants. When the boy fails to get free, then, Blake says he learns to sulk. When a man sulks he becomes passive to his own hurts."[1]

He remains trapped before the first gate, in other words, a "mama's boy" unable to face his fears and escape from her, even though he knows that she cheated him of a father and, of course, he will never trust her again or, by association, any woman. And so the family curse is carried forward.

Despite the emotional stranglehold of the controlling mother, the child in this situation will still feel himself an orphan because that is in the nature of his script. How this manifests is apparent. Some years ago, psychologists got a number of people, all strangers to each other, together at a cocktail party and simply stood back and watched their interactions. When they looked at the results, they found an interesting correlation between the family histories of their party guests and the connections they made at the party. The youngest daughter from one family would introduce herself to the youngest daughter from another, for example, even though they had no prior knowledge of each other, as none of the guests did. At the end of the evening only a few people had made no contacts with any others. The psychologists did not understand why until they looked at the history of this subgroup. They were all orphans.[2] There is nothing in the rulebook that says orphans cannot mix with people at a party, of course, but every one of them knew instinctively that their curse was to be alone, just as Eli's was.[3]

The second alternative for the "orphan son"—and the most likely outcome for any son worth his salt—is to reject the mother and the script she has imposed on him when the extent of her controlling personality is revealed. With this response he is able to burst through his fears and become a Seeker after truth, finding freedom for himself and from the family curse.

"What does the son do?" writes Bly. "He turns away . . . goes outside to feed with wild things, lives among dens and huts, eats distance and silence; he grows long wings, enters the spiral, ascends."[4]

"That's the origin of the myth 'young man, go find your father,'" writes Joseph Campbell—so you can finally know the truth of who you are.[5]

We all operate under such life scripts and, if you look back at the cues your parents gave you, it is probably no surprise that you are seeking power (or giving it away) in whatever way you are—as a doctor, lawyer, entrepreneur, or the bagman for an East End gang.

We may be through with the past, but the past ain't through with us.

—FROM THE FILM, *MAGNOLIA*

We explore this further in the next exercise.

EXERCISE 10

Your Life Mission

Lie down, relax, and breathe deeply into your abdomen for a count of four, hold for a count of four, then release for a count of four. This pattern is known as four-way breathing and will help to calm and still you. Repeat the pattern a few times, then forget about it and let your breathing take care of itself.

*Stage 1: The Child's Vision**

Close your eyes and see yourself, as you are now, walking into a deep cave that descends into the Earth. You feel quite safe here; in fact, it is comforting to be in this place.

---

*Parts of this meditation are based on the GUTS training developed by Steve Kushner of the Shadow Healing Community (see www.shadowhealing.com).

Ahead of you, you see daylight where the tunnel ends. Beyond it is an open field. Walk toward the light and step out onto the grass. Look around. Take your time.

You begin to sense that you are not alone here, and your eye is drawn to a small figure on the horizon. You walk in that direction and, as you get closer, notice that the figure is that of a child, probably no older than five, who is sitting on the grass, hunched forward, gently crying.

As you draw close and look into the face of this child, you realize it is yourself you are looking at: a younger you who is upset at something that is taking place in his or her life. Sit down too and begin to comfort the child. He or she is delighted to see you and relaxes in your presence.

"What can I do to make things better for you?" you ask. "If you had a single wish that could change things and make a better world for you, what would it be? What would your vision of a perfect world look like?"

The child thinks for a while and then answers you. "My perfect world would be . . ."

Open your eyes and write down or draw the child's answer.

If you had to summarize this vision of a perfect world in just one word, what would it be?

Write it down here: _____

Stage 2: Saving the Child

Now close your eyes and relax again. Allow yourself to drift back to that field beyond the cave and to your younger self. "I understand your vision," you say. "Now, what can I do to make it real for you? What actions do I need to take to make this vision happen?"

The child is silent for a moment and then answers you: "These are the actions I'd like you to take . . ."

Acknowledge what he or she is telling you and remember it. If you are inspired to do so, make the child a promise that you will do what it takes to create this more perfect world.

Spend some time with the child now, having fun, connecting, making a bond between you. Then, when you are ready to leave, hug him or her to you and tell them that you love them.

As you do so, something remarkable happens. It is as if this boy or girl, now joyful and secure in your company, becomes a child of mist, of energy, pure spirit, and this mist is absorbed within you at your heart. You feel it entering you, filling you with childlike joy. And suddenly you two are one.

You turn and walk back across the field to the cave, through the tunnel, back to your room, your body, and to full consciousness, feeling invigorated, energized, and wide awake.

Open your eyes and write down or draw the child's answer to your question: "What actions do I need to take to make your vision real?"

What are these actions needed to make a perfect world? If you had to summarize them as a single word, what would it be?

Write it down here: _____

Stage 3: What Is Your Purpose in Life?

You should now have two words in front of you—one a *vision* word and one an *action* word. Use these to complete the sentence below by inserting them in the appropriate places.

"My purpose in life is to create _____
[vision word] by acting with _____[action word] toward others."

(So, for example, your statement might read: "My purpose is to create *happiness* by acting with *kindness* toward others.")

By exploring your unconscious connections to a time before your own "family curse" really took hold in your psyche, what you now have in front of you is your purest mission in life; the thing you most need to know as a Seeker after purpose and the thing that you came here to do.

Stage 4: Your Secret Self

There is more to this exercise, however, because what you also just did was trick your rational mind (which would normally protect you from such information) into allowing you access to two of your own best-kept secrets.

To understand the first of these secrets, rewrite your purpose to reflect its exact opposite. So, using the example above ("My purpose in life is to create *happiness* by acting with *kindness* toward others"), the rewriting would be: "My purpose in life is to create *unhappiness* by acting with *unkindness* toward others." This new sentence is a reflection of your shadow self. This is most likely also how you are using your Seeker energy in the pursuit of personal power, during your more unconscious moments.

Our shadow selves are the ones we have been taught by society to use when we go after power. They are revealed in our ambitions to win, to "get to the top," to have authority over others in business, leadership, or love, during all of those times when we are not really thinking for ourselves.

Now that you see your shadow, you can, if you wish, change it. If that is your desire, what I'd like to propose is that you do two things:

First, reflect for a while on the times you have acted from your shadow in pursuit of power, so you become aware of the situations in which your shadow self is most likely to emerge. In other words: using our example, those times when you did *not* create happiness because you acted unkindly or without full consciousness, even though you may not have intended it. Knowledge of these things is also power.

Second, make a commitment to change: whenever these situations arise again you will do something to break the pattern, even if it is only walking away. Sometimes leaving the scene is a more genuine act of kindness and courage than staying with good intentions and allowing the shadow to take over.

Stage 5: Revealing the Curse

To explore the second of these inner secrets, I ask you to accept the possibility that the positive mission statement you wrote *is* your jubaku or "family curse," when looked at in a certain way.

We are driven to change the things in our lives that cause us harm or discomfort. This is only natural, a basic survival instinct. What we also know is that we are creatures prone to projection, with rational minds that will try to protect us from harm—and from truth—at every turn. What you have written may therefore be a projection in itself. It is written in terms of making the world a better place. But isn't it actually an insight into your life and the things *you* need to change so you can stand in your own authentic power?

Look again at the statement you wrote and ask yourself, "Who did not act toward me in the way I have described?" So, in our example, you would ask, Who was it that did not make me happy? Who acted unkindly and unconsciously toward me?

Whoever they were or are, they are likely to be people instrumental in your jubaku or geis and one of the reasons you are seeking power and purpose in the way you are. Spend a little time reflecting on this new information and then close this book. Do not come back to it for nine days—or until you are prepared to forgive that person. You don't have to be *ready* to forgive them, just *prepared* to.

By *forgive*, I mean let go of the drama that surrounds them—not in some saintly way and not even for their sake, but for your own. While you are still involved in the past, you cannot move forward into a new future. When you let go of the past, however, you can move on and have the things you want.

There is an exercise to help you with this in the next chapter. For now, just close this book and think about it.

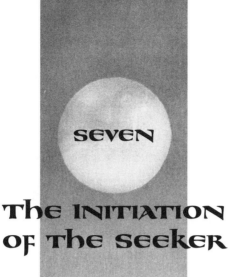

SEVEN

The Initiation
of the Seeker

Techniques for Recovering Power
and Finding Purpose

*As far as we can discern, the sole purpose of human existence is
to kindle a light of meaning in the darkness of mere being.*

—CARL JUNG

The Ninja knew that loss of power
is never a one-way street. We *allow* others to take our power. To do so
we must be in agreement with them in some way, that we will accept
their definitions of us and of what power means. We must also agree to
the rewards we believe they offer us—acceptance, security, love, purpose, belonging, or whatever—in return for giving up our power, even
though the manifestation of these "rewards" (status, fame, wealth, etc.)
are themselves illusory and often do not serve us.

In warrior terms, we are willing to give power away because of our
"self-importance." This does not imply arrogance or big-headedness;
rather, it means that our ego-selves have been conditioned to place us at
the center of every drama, whether the drama itself is positive or negative, helpful or harmful. It doesn't matter, in other words, whether we
see ourselves as the heroes or villains, victims or rescuers of the piece; it
is seeing ourselves in a role *at all*—our acceptance of the circumstances

103

and the label that goes with it—that holds us in a prison of our own making, attached to things that bring us pleasure *and* pain, and separate from the natural flow of the universe.

This duality and separation into "Us and Them," "I and That," underlies all life games or issues that have to do with power. We crave attention or recognition from others because that is what we have been taught to look for, and so we become addicted to compliments and insults, accomplishments and failures, as a way of demonstrating who we are to ourselves and others. If nothing else, the attention proves that we are alive. Since there is no absolute indicator of success or failure, however, enough is never enough, and we find ourselves in search of the unattainable—because, ultimately, only *we* can know if we are "good (or bad) enough"; there is no one else who can tell us.

While we see ourselves as separate from the flow of the universe, we can never be *in* that flow; while we see ourselves as Seekers *after* power, we can never *have* that power. As soon as we let go of our self-importance, however, we find ourselves attached to nothing and at one with everything, and then all things are possible. "How do you find anything that's lost?" John Locke asks in the ABC series, *Lost:* "You stop looking for it."

When we abandon labels and limitations, we allow ourselves the opportunity for a power that may be immense.

Petty Tyrants

If, however, we make the mistake of seeking purpose and acceptance from another person, then we feed that person our power and we feed off of theirs, becoming characters in the drama of their lives, as they are in ours. This can be serious when the person at the center of that drama is a Petty Tyrant, because there is no more ruthless thief of power. Paradoxically, however, a good Petty Tyrant can also be one of our greatest allies for reclaiming power.

The Ninja knew real tyrants. The philosophy was born at a time when Japan was composed of many feudal states, with frequent wars and needless waste of life, as local warlords battled for power. Although the times were hard and the blood spilled freely on the land, there is an argument to be made that the Ninja would never have learned their craft without the tyranny around them that made their skills necessary.

Although we do not find ourselves today at the mercy of feudal warlords in quite the same way as the Ninja, we are still beset by their modern equivalents: Petty Tyrants—those annoying, irritating, demanding, or underhanded people who push our buttons, knock us off balance, and make us lose our cool. They range in type and persona from petty bureaucrats who hold us back and smother us in red tape to aggressive bullies who present a serious threat to our health and happiness. They can be minor irritants or a major pain in the ass, but in all cases they leave us feeling disempowered, drawn into their dramas, and forced to see the world through their eyes, because there is hardly ever room for negotiation or compromise with a tyrant.

For example, two of the Petty Tyrants we have surely all met are the Critic and the Victim. The Critic is a shadow of the Magus (see chapter 8). All bureaucrats, in their fixation on rules and procedures, have something of the Critic about them. In more mundane circumstances, he or she is also the nag for whom nothing you do is ever right or enough.

Critics are slaves to their minds, which are always eddying around looking for new faults to pick on. The ungrateful boss, the partner or parent who harangues you constantly, are examples of this sort of person. They will wear you down, chipping away at you for as long as you stay in their orbit, until you eventually surrender and begin living by their rules.

You have two strategies for dealing with Critics. Because they are enslaved by their minds, your first option is to use the tools of the mind—reason and analysis—to take their arguments apart. Emotional appeals rarely work. Assuming you are in the right, the Critic has little defense against a counterargument that follows his or her own rules and logic. Your other option is to quietly stand your ground and refuse to budge on anything the Critic says to you. The pure Critic, seeing that you are incapable of rational thought, will not waste energy on you for long.

The Victim/Martyr, now, is a different thing entirely. You might think it unfair to call someone who has been victimized a tyrant. That is often the power of the Victim for drawing you into his or her game. Victims are expert dramatists who, without even appealing to you directly, can get you on their side and offering to sort out their problems (i.e., giving away your power) in a matter of minutes.

Victims appeal to your emotions and sense of pity. They look for rescuers (attention) because they have not dealt with their own issues of power or power loss. In order to be "saved" (fed with power) they must therefore also attract persecutors (another form of attention). Then there is always a drama to be saved from and someone to save them from it. In this way, they drain power from both sides at once. (Eli's case study in chapter 6 is an example of how this drama might play itself out, with real and unfortunate consequences for those around the Victim.)

Rapunzel is a classic fairy tale example. In the story, the beautiful child with the golden hair is locked up in a tower by an evil witch (the persecutor) and saved by a handsome prince (the rescuer) who implores her to "let down her hair" so he can climb it and be at her side. There then ensues a whole drama of plots and counterplots, witch against prince and prince versus witch, while Rapunzel merely sits back and watches. It never seems to have occurred to Rapunzel to do something for herself, or to the lovesick and hypnotized prince to end all this pala-ver by simply standing beneath the tower and shouting "Rapunzel, for God's sake jump!" Instead, he goes along with her drama, ending up wounded and blind as a consequence.

In a final twist, once the prince is disabled, Rapunzel miraculously discovers her own freedom and seeks her hero out so she can then take care of him (thereby turning him into a Victim as well), and they both live unhappily ever after, with her no doubt complaining behind his back about the extra burden she now has of caring for a man who is blind.

This is the power of a Victim, who has the ability to draw you in and stab you in the back (or, if you are a handsome prince, have your eyes torn out with thorns)—but can never actually be helped. The game of a Victim is to stay a Victim, so they cannot allow themselves to be res-cued, or remain with one persecutor for long, because once "seen," their methods become obvious. Victims need to remain in mystery in order to be empowered and then disempowered again. The Victim's strategy for living, in fact, corresponds to the "five feelings" identified in the Ninja *gojo* (model of emotional motivations used for defeating an enemy): vanity, anger, soft-heartedness, laziness, and cowardice.

Your best strategy with a Victim is to discuss his problems objectively with him, as well as his possible solutions, and be prepared to leave it at that. If he truly wants a resolution to his problems, he then has the tools he needs and can get on with it. The worst thing you can do is sort out his problems for him. He will not grow from this and you will be labeled by him as "controlling," since this is one of the few words and emotional states a Victim genuinely understands.

We can treat Petty Tyrants like this either as enemies to be resisted or avoided, or as teachers to be learned from, and, significantly, as mirrors to ourselves and sources of useful information, as they reveal to us our real enemies—those within.

Ninja philosophy states that the tyrants we attract into our lives are there for a reason. We feel an affinity with them in some way, and they stand as reflections of ourselves. So whoever it is that is upsetting you in whatever way, it is worth pausing to ask yourself what buttons they are actually pushing, which nerves they are getting on—and whether you recognize their behavior in yourself. The answer is probably yes. This is the gift of the Tyrant: he or she allows us to discover new things about ourselves and the circumstances, situations, or people we most often give our power away to. A skillful response to them therefore allows us to reclaim power for ourselves.

Lucy, a client of mine, was having problems with her brother-in-law, for example. Whenever they met they would end up arguing, and Lucy found him aggressive and judgmental toward her. Most recently, they had argued about modern science, of all things! Her brother-in-law's view was that science had the answer to everything and that all things in the universe are known. Lucy's view was the opposite: that nothing can be fully known because even science discovers new things each day and changes its opinions as often.

We decided to accept her brother-in-law as a Petty Tyrant for the purpose of our therapy session, and Lucy and I looked at what this argument might really be about. What it came down to was this: her brother-in-law was afraid of freedom. He needed his universe to be known and ordered to the point of regimentation, and science was his savior in this, offering a watertight container for an otherwise chaotic world. Lucy could see this was true of him and, having understood that his aggressively stated opinions were really a mask for his fear, she was able to take back her power and stop being afraid of his outbursts. Indeed, she now felt quite sorry for him.

Even more useful, though, was the fact that her brother-in-law was a perfect and opposite mirror for Lucy herself. She craved freedom rather than constraint and was fearful of being trapped in a world where everything was known. This would be stifling for her, and this is what science represented. From this seemingly trivial observation, we were given a massive kick-start for the therapy, because one of Lucy's key issues had already been identified: fear of being held in and held back. We were then able to look at where this came from, which led to further insights about her childhood, her life script, her home life and relationships. All of these insights came in rapid succession and in one therapy session we were able to do the work of three weeks under normal circumstances—all thanks to her brother-in-law.

Indeed, so useful are Petty Tyrants in this respect that many warrior schools advise their students to go out and find one for themselves, as spiritual progress is usually more rapid with input from these worthy opponents.

EXERCISE 11

The People Who Press Your Buttons

We are most irritated by (and therefore give our power away to) the people who most remind us of the faults or issues we see in ourselves. Knowing this, we can use our Tyrants to gain insight into ourselves and take back the power we have invested in these external people and things.

Close your eyes and breathe slowly and deeply. Allow an image to form of a magical mirror that will show you the truth of yourself. In this mirror, an image appears of someone who annoys or irritates you, causes you some sort of conflict or pain in life, or pushes your buttons in some other way. It may not be the person you expected to see.

Once this image has formed, ask that person, "In what ways am I exactly like you?" Then listen to what he or she has to say. Thank the person for the information and wish them well, then breathe out and open your eyes. Make a note of what you have learned. These are the lessons you need to apply to your life in order to be free.

Losing Power and Getting It Back

We can lose—or give away—our power in so many ways that it is impossible to enumerate them all. They range from the trauma of dealing unskillfully with our Petty Tyrants (that is, giving in to their apparent power instead of using them as opportunities for growth), to the experience of lost love, where we move into harmony with another and then watch that person leave, taking a part of us with her when she goes. Consider this though: whatever happened *has* happened. It is gone. At a physical level, you are somebody new. As I wrote in a previous book, by the time you get to the period at the end of this sentence, one hundred thousand cells in your body will have died and been replaced.[1] All the protein in your body is lost and renewed every thirty days. Multiply that by the number of days, weeks, months, or years since the traumatic event and you can see that you *now* is not you *then*. Not even physically. You are wiser, more powerful and able. Whatever it was, you survived it. As the philosopher Neitzsche said, whatever does not kill us makes us stronger.

What is it that keeps us tied to the emotional hurts or habits of the past when, physically, we are brand new people? The answer is that, though our cells may get replaced, there is something within us that endures and carries its experiences forward. That something is the ego.

It is the continuation of us, the why-we-don't-forget who we have been, even as we evolve into brand new people with every breath we take.

The ego keeps us attached to long-gone pains, holding us in prisons of the past through our agreement to listen to its continuous chatter of guilt, shame, and the allocation of blame. It is a drain on our power, the voice of our self-importance. Our continual rebirth, second-on-second, as constantly evolving human beings, meanwhile, gives us new opportunities to break free from the past by making a conscious commitment to do so.

One of the ways we retreat into pain and deny ourselves power is by clinging to the promises we have made to others, which we could never hope to keep. Such promises are common in emotional relationships where power is involved—"I'll never forget you"/"I'll never forgive you," "I owe you everything"/"I owe you nothing," "You are my life"/"I'll get by just fine without you." With these pronouncements we allow our egos to speak for us as shields for our vulnerability.

We repeat these promises unthinkingly in the flush of new love or a relationship's end, without consciously assessing their true implications for us and for others. Our emotional selves then accept these words as instructions and we become bound by them. We do not stay fluid and dynamic but are hooked by events from our history.

As soon as we decide to take back our power from such false promises, we give ourselves the freedom to live more authentically from now on. We also ensure that we never make the same mistakes again, because now we can make real promises, conscious ones, with full awareness of who we are and hope to be.

If you are living with such an attachment to the past, here is an exercise for reclaiming power.

EXERCISE 12

Cutting Ties to the Past

It is impossible to be present if you're trapped in personal history. And what, after all, is the difference between the past and a dream?

—RAM DASS

Before they went into battle, the Ninja warriors had a meditation they performed. They would draw their swords from their sheaths and hold the blades in front of them. Then they would visualize all of their fears, their attachments to life, their times of *muryoku* (powerlessness) becoming solid on the tip of the sword. These things became like a poison that would infect the enemy whenever the sword cut. The intention was for the warrior to go into battle pure, fighting not for himself (which would lack giri—honor) but for the good of the clan. To strike down an enemy in anger was considered an impure act. Warriors did what they had to do; they did not fight because of emotional attachments or a desire for victory, they fought for freedom.

This meditation is an adaptation of that technique.

Close your eyes, breathe into your heart, and see yourself with someone you have made a promise to in the past and who, through this gesture, you still feel attached to, even though the relationship itself has ended. In this image, see yourself and the other person sitting together in an empty room. Within this room you (but not the other) also sit within a spiral of protective energy that separates you both.

Look at your bodies and you will see that strands of energy connect you, from your body to his or hers. Notice where these strands connect. This will show you the deeper relationship that existed between you. Is it a heart connection? Sexual? Of the mind? Notice also if there is a discrepancy in where these strands connect (e.g., do they leave your body at the heart but connect to his at the head?). This can suggest where miscommunication is taking place in your relationships or provide insight into where and how your power is taken by others. (Lucy, for example—whom we met earlier in the chapter—carried out this exercise to explore her relationship to her brother-in-law and saw strands of energy emerging from his mouth but attaching to her solar plexus, the place where she experienced emotional hurt in her body. His words were what caused her discomfort and, knowing that this was his strategy for provoking fear and taking power from her, she now had a way of dealing with it and with him—by simply not listening to him!)

When you are ready, say whatever needs to be said to the person in front of you, speaking out loud, so you can forgive or make amends, accept that person's forgiveness, finish your business together, take back your promises, and say goodbye.

When the time is right, you will see in your hand a sword you can use to cut the ties of energy between you. Breathe in as you do so to reclaim the power that was yours. This does not hurt the other or you; you are simply cutting through energy.

As you free them and yourself from the past, watch the other person drift away from you, becoming more distant until they fade away completely. Gently open your eyes and say out loud "I am free"—and commit to that sentiment.

Psychologists call such exercises systematic desensitization and use them often in the treatment of phobias, where we give away power to an irrational fear. In simple terms, they are a way of rehearsing our taking back of power: the more we are exposed safely to a person or situation that has been stealing power from us, the stronger and less fearful of that person we become.

Repeat this exercise whenever you need to and for every situation in which you feel you gave away your power.

What's the Worst that Could Happen?

The biggest problem for people in using their power is often the fear of what might happen if they did. When our ties with the past are cut, for example, it may feel lonely, as if our old pain were actually a friend or a form of support for us, and now we are alone and the future is uncertain. In a recent workshop, just before we began a series of power retrieval exercises, I asked the group to imagine the worst thing that could possibly happen if they were fully in their power and could have anything they set their minds to. Two answers stand out, one from a female participant: "I'd be happy," and one from a male: "I'd get what I want." These, for them, were the *worst* things that could happen. It might seem bizarre that people should come to a workshop to recover their power and yet be afraid of doing so, but I hear such statements all the time. As Thich Nhat Hanh wrote: "People have a hard time letting go of their suffering. Out of a fear of the unknown, they prefer suffering that is familiar."[2]

There is a reason for this, as the following exercise may show you.

EXERCISE 13

The Worst-Case Scenario

Close your eyes, breathe deeply, relax, and ask yourself, "What is the worst that could happen now that I have committed to taking back my power?" Another form of this question might be: "What is the worst that could happen if I had all the power, abilities, and talents to be as free and happy as I want?" or ". . . if I had the single thing I most want or need in my life?" Let an image form in your mind's eye of this "worst thing."

You might find, in one way or another, that the answer comes back to responsibility. Freedom must be fought for, and authentic power always comes with real responsibility. The worst that could happen, then, is that we must be warriors, accountable for our actions and for achieving the things we desire.

Breathe out when you are ready and open your eyes. Now you know the "worst": that we all have to be real—and actually that's not so bad. *The worst that could happen is we become who we already are.*

Water: The Second Ally

Shinto, a philosophy at the heart of Ninja spirituality, has as one of its key teachings that nature is sacred. To be immersed in nature is to be close to the gods, and all around us there are *kami* (nature spirits)—in the landscape, in the leaves and the breeze, in the plane where our breath meets the air. Everything is alive and we are always in the presence of the sacred.

Warriors throughout history have therefore learned about themselves through their observations of nature. Since all things are connected, whatever they find there they also find in themselves. Through the peace that nature brings, they also arrive at *makoto*—the true heart or, we might also say, sincerity: what is real.

Water (sui) is our ally within the Godai for dealing with the emotions and matters of power. Observe the tides of the ocean—the ebb and flow, forward and backward, on and on. The message of Water is that all is movement, all is in flow. There are no frozen waves, just as there are no frozen feelings. It is only when we allow ourselves to form attachments to events and definitions that we become frozen in time and our emotions become fixed. It is in these moments that we lose our power.

Stand on a beach sometime and watch the waves. You will find that a pattern emerges: a number of smaller waves and then a larger one that crashes onto the shore. So it is with our emotions: a series of small events that eventually lead to one big reaction. If we can control the smaller things, or transform their energy, then the big event—the one that causes us pain or anger, depression or despair—the loss of power—might never happen.

EXERCISE 14

Understanding Your Emotions

One way to understand your emotions is to keep a journal, an emotional logbook, for a period of one month. Decide which emotion you want to look at—anger, sorrow, joy, and so on—and work with one emotion at a time, remembering of course that all of these are really just labels for an experience; they are not the event itself. Then make a note, with date and time, of each occasion that you have this emotion arising.

Ask yourself these questions:

What prompted this emotion?

What was happening?

What was said?

Who was with me?

What was going through my mind—and my body?

What did I do?

Complete the record in as much detail as you can every time this emotion comes up. Then, at the end of the month, go back over your journal and note the common threads between events. Is there any thing or situation in particular that prompted these emotional responses? It is to these things that you have a tendency to give up your power.

Now look back over your life. Is there a singular event, a first memory, something that was done or said that links all of these situations together? That is the situation in which your power was first taken and an energetic attachment was made to those and similar circumstances.

Now that you see this, repeat Exercise 12, cutting your attachments to this first event and releasing it.

Ichimonji No Kamae: Water Movement

The Ninja body movement for experiencing the Water state is *ichimonji no kamae*. This reflects the fluidity of Water and of the emotions—"a flexible, elusive feeling."[3]

Begin with your left leg forward, knee slightly bent, and your right leg behind you, also bent. Your front foot points forward while your back foot points to the side, so your feet are in an L shape. The right (back) leg carries most of your weight.

Your body is angled toward your imaginary adversary (the person or emotional state that is stealing your power). Your left arm is extended in front of you, fingers pointing forward; your right arm is across your chest, fingers almost touching your left shoulder.

Now imagine that your opponent moves toward you. You react fluidly, receding backward from their attack, unavailable to them. As you do so, swap your arms so that the right extends forward while the left crosses over your chest. Your legs also change, stepping back on the left so that the right now leads. Both actions are taken at the same time and at a gentle pace, like that of t'ai chi. Keep moving slowly backward in this way, exhausting your opponent while you conserve your power.

When you feel the time is right, like the sea crashing ahead to the shore, change direction and move quickly forward, striking through your opponent with your leading hand. In your mind's eye, see all your emotional connections dissolve as you cut through their hold over you and take back your power.

EXERCISE 15
Cloud Gazing and Water Breathing: Sensing the Flow

There are no fixed patterns and no absolute emotions. We only think there are. This is a gentle meditation that allows you to see that all things are relative and in flow, not fixed at all. We can always change. We can be in our power.

Find a peaceful place outdoors where you can lie on your back and simply gaze up at the clouds, Water drifting across the sky. You will see all sorts of shapes in the clouds and your mind will create patterns. That is absolutely a man's face; this is absolutely a dog, a tree, a mountain. And yet, as you continue to gaze, all of those "absolutes" change and fade as the clouds take on new shapes and become something else. So it is with life and with you. There are no absolutes. You can change. We all can. We already are.

As you look skyward, something else may also occur to you. It is as if you are looking down rather than up. You could be on clouds made of Earth looking down at an Earth made of sky. *Clouds* and *Earth* are just words. The truth is that there is no up and no down; we are all just floating in space. In fact, are you dreaming these clouds or are they dreaming you?

Combine this meditation with a breathing exercise—the Breath of Water. Slowly and gently take four short inward breaths, like sipping air; hold the breath for two seconds and then release it in one longer out-breath. Like waves moving out to sea and returning to the shore.

As you exhale see all your cares and concerns leaving your body, carried by your breath up into the clouds and away. No fixed patterns at all.

WARRIOR COMMITMENT

I Step into Power and Become the Seeker
I am the flow of the universe and, like all things, I am fluid and available to change.

I maintain my power by letting go of attachments that do not serve or concern me. I invest in authentic power by placing my energies where they best serve my needs.

Like the tides, I move backward out of reach of conflict, and forward with full commitment once my decisions are made.

I know that all things are transient and my emotions are just descriptions of the world. I choose freedom and happiness as my descriptions of this mysterious world that I create for myself, and I accept responsibility for ensuring that things are this way.

I make this commitment to myself with full consciousness, as a gesture of power, and to honor myself.

I let this commitment go to the universe, and I believe and trust that things will be this way.

SIGNED: _____

DATE: _____

INTO Thin AIR

A bit of advice given to a young Native American at the time of his initiation: "As you go the way of life, you will see a great chasm. Jump. It's not as wide as you think."

—JOSEPH CAMPBELL

On the day you die, the breeze on your cheek may be the sweetest thing. The smell of heather or the feel of the Earth may be your most sensational memory. Or that is my experience, at least.

Forget who you were, the things you've been through, all you thought you'd be remembered for. At the moment of your death you are a fleeting thing. You will vanish into time, swallowed by the soil and turned into memory, which may be of you, but is never really ever who you were. People need myths to live by and that is what you become. Someone else's interpretation of your life takes over. In the memories and myths of others you may become a giant or a dwarf—a loving mother or a control freak who smothered her kids; a business titan or a lonely man who abandoned his family for work. All of that is out of your control. But one thing is certain: you will not be *you*. So you may as well let go of your image and beliefs about yourself now. Get out of your mind and stop creating yourself in someone else's words.

You realize this when you are standing blindfold at the edge of a cliff, and your teacher is telling you to jump into what you know is a 200-foot drop to a hard quarry floor. You know in that instant before you jump that, actually, it doesn't matter how you're remembered because once you're gone you can't control anything anymore. But then, once you're gone you don't need to. If only we could live our lives like that, with freedom from "who we are."

At the end of one of Castaneda's books, don Juan takes him to the edge of a deep ravine to demonstrate, dramatically, that the whole world is illusion, a product of the mind, and that everyone and everything is comprised of energy or essence, not image and persona.

Castaneda, a scientist, has heard this message many times but has always rationalized it and turned it into theory instead of fact so it will fit his scientific model of the world. It is only when don Juan takes him to the cliff edge and tells him they are going to jump that he begins to see the relevance of the teachings he has heard. Because now it is life or death. Castaneda will either dematerialize his physical body (possible, perhaps, if the world and everything in it is comprised of energy), veto his rational mind, and "stop the world," or he will die. It will be—literally—a leap of faith that other descriptions of the world are possible.

And so he jumps—just as the Shugendo warriors jumped into their abysses and for the same reasons: to challenge their perceptions of what is real.

And that is why I find myself here today, taking the same leap of faith. My teacher tells me to clasp my arms in front of me "like an arrow, pointing toward the flaming heart of the sun," to gather my power, and then jump into the abyss.

All I *can* do is jump, because that is what I am committed to. And so I leap, head first, arms out straight in front of me, hands clasped together as if in prayer. The breeze on my cheek is the sweetest thing on Earth.*

---

*The Leap of Faith is an occasional workshop I run that is based on this practice of "jumping into the abyss." See www.VodouShaman.com for details.

eight

FU (AIR): The Magus Facing Confusion

Faith Versus "Truth"

Faith is stronger than so-called reality.
—Herman Hesse

Our journey of initiation through the Ninja gateways of fear and power brings us to the place of the west and the archetypal energy of the Magus. We now have courage and authentic power on our side. We also know something of our purpose. The work of initiation in the west is to apply these gifts and find a vision for our lives which is *makoto*—"real" or "sincere."

The importance of such a vision was paramount to the Ninja, and it should not be underestimated by us in the modern West if we are to be healthy individuals acting from a sense of meaning, clear identity, and well-being. An opinion poll in France found that 89 percent of the people were desperate for something real to believe in. A study of nearly eight thousand Americans found similar results: 78 percent still needed to find "purpose and meaning to my life."[1]

Having such a vision can be vital to our survival. Viktor Frankl, a psychiatrist who survived the Auschwitz and Dachau death camps, wrote of prisoners who allowed themselves to die in captivity "because [they] could not see any future goal . . . everything in a way became pointless." Once a man reached this stage of no-vision, his death was assured. There was even a recognizable process to it. For a few days, the prisoner would become obsessed with the past, the life he had left behind; then one morning he would refuse to get up for work, inviting punishment from the guards or even execution. A little later he would reach into his pocket and bring out his last cigarette, smoking this hard-earned luxury saved for some future celebration, as if in a trance. In most cases by morning he would be dead, having simply lost the will to live.

"Any attempt to restore man's inner strength in the camp had first to succeed in showing him some future goal," Frankl wrote. "Nietzsche's words, 'He who has a *why* to live for can bear with almost any *how*,' could be the guiding motto."[2] Without a vision to our life, we invite our spiritual or even our physical death.

The task of the warrior is to find this vision. Our enemy is confusion as we struggle to do so (see Kevin's story in chapter 2). Our reward, if we make it, is clarity, the ability to unravel the mysteries of life, to know more about ourselves, and to focus on the things we really want instead of carrying our past around with us like a heavy rucksack onto the myriad paths of our possible futures. The challenge for the Magus—the one who truly sees—is to understand and accept that the world is an act of faith, not a "known fact," and that there are no cut-and-dried answers or final solutions.

Despite all the things we were brought up to accept and the rules we have been asked to live by, we still stand at the heart of a mystery by virtue, simply, of taking part in this adventure of discovery that is our lives. Those at the initiatory gateway between clarity and confusion will find themselves at a place of self-reflection where questions about what is "true" and "real" become important. If they can make the transition, they will have new vision and direction in life; if not, they may meet the shadow of the Magus: bewilderment and aloneness, a feeling of being lost, and, because of this, the temptation to turn down their dreams.

It takes some time to see through the illusion of our "taken-for-granteds" in life, so this initiatory step normally comes at the middle stage of any endeavor, when we have some track record behind us but are not yet at the end of the journey. It is at these times that a healthy self-doubt creeps in and we need a period of reflection. The midpoint of a relationship where we need to commit or split, and a work project where we must allocate resources or cut our losses, are examples of such middle stages when we need to look at where we've been and use our knowledge to inform the future. It is also there in middle age—the classic "mid-life crisis"—when we can look back over twenty or thirty years of building a career, earning money, gaining promotions, buying houses, raising families—and realize that this is not actually feeding our souls; there must be more to life than this.

The real choice modern initiates must then make is between "truth" and "faith." The world of social convention has been presented to them as the only truth for the whole of their lives, but it no longer seems to work. This heralds its own confusion. After all, any truth must be fixed, solid, immutable, or else it is not truth but opinion (at best) or fiction (in absolute terms). With this realization the warrior begins to understand that he or she has always been living an act of faith, not truth: faith that the world really is the way it has been presented, and that its values are his. The warrior understands now that he has spent part of his life pursuing a fantasy and that he has a choice: to give up on himself, forget his doubts and continue this fiction, or to give up the act and be true to himself so he can give birth to a new life.

For the warrior, this is not a choice at all.

Acting is the expression of a neurotic impulse. . . .
Quitting acting, that's the sign of maturity.

—MARLON BRANDO

The Truth About Truth

Can You Believe the Evividence of Your Own Eyes?

truth. *n.* Quality or state of being true or accurate or honest . . .
accurate. *a.* In exact conformity with a standard or with truth . . .
honest. *a.* Not lying . . .

—CONCISE OXFORD DICTIONARY

These definitions say almost nothing about one of the single most important concepts in the modern world. The pursuit of truth is, after all, what our legal systems are based on; it is what makes a country a democracy; it is fundamental to our religions; it is at the heart of our educational system. Without truth, how can any of these things survive? There has to be "right" and "wrong." Doesn't there?

Given the importance of this concept, we might at least expect clarity about what it is we're looking for. But let's go back to those definitions. *Truth* is about being accurate and honest; *accuracy* is about the "truth"; *honesty* is about not lying—in other words, telling the truth. The whole thing is, at best, tautological. In fact, it tells us nothing.

What we consider to be true, by and large, are the things we witness with our own eyes. And yet, we have been so indoctrinated into the ways and values of the world, that we cannot reliably trust even these. The Ninja realized this and perfected combat strategies for making the most of such human weaknesses, such as *yukigakurejutsu* (the art of "hiding in snow"—making ourselves appear as something else) and *kyojutsu ten kan* (the philosophical art of treating truth as deception, and vice versa). The studies of modern-day psychologists into eyewitness reports give credence to the utility of this approach.

Imagine that you saw a crime taking place. Adrenalin would flood your system, your senses would be hyper-alert, and you would take notice of everything that happened. And yet, when psychologists looked at more than two hundred cases of wrongful arrest, the cause of the mistake was unreliable eyewitness testimonies in more than half (52 percent) of cases. There is a good chance that no matter how alert you were, you would still get it wrong.[3]

One reason for this is that our memory of what we see or experience is not fixed, but flowing and dynamic like everything else in life, and just as capable of change. Every memory we have requires an effort toward meaning—a search for the truth—to make sense of that event. Personal history is what we use to give us this sense of what happened, and so every memory is a combination of our previous experience and our beliefs about how things *should* be (mental habits, in other words).

Psychological research suggests that we ignore things that don't fit our pre-existing ideas and only remember "main meanings," rather than specifics. You might know the basic plot of your life—your life script—for example, but you will not recall all the events that took place to get you where you are now.

But in that case—if your memory is so selective in this way—do you really know who you are at all? Do you even have this life script, or are you just agreeing to buy into it? "Is all that we see or seem just a dream within a dream?" as Edgar Allen Poe phrased this question. The answer, more than likely, is yes.

I had a student in a workshop once, Martin, who volunteered for a demonstration about life mission work and the jubaku (family curse) he felt himself to be living (see chapter 6). His life mission, he said, was "to create stability in the world."

Martin and I stood at the center of the group and he picked out a participant to represent his mother and one to represent his father, both of whom joined us in the center. I then asked him to have his "parents" speak the sort of words they would normally use when they reflected to him their feelings about the world "out there." "The world is a fearful place," his "father" intoned over and over. "The world is beautiful—but listen to what your father says," said his "mother."

What Martin wanted most from the world was stability—and it is not hard to see why when you consider the schizophrenic message he got from his parents. How different the world would have been for Martin, how different his life would have been, and how differently he would have noticed things as an eyewitness of life if he had chosen to listen to his mother ("life is beautiful") instead of his father ("the world is fearful")—or if his mother had not added the instruction that Martin should heed his father and ignore what she was saying. Those six little words—"listen to what your father says"—changed his perceptions of life, because he now regarded the world as unstable (a judgment he had applied to it) and saw everything in those terms, instead of appreciating it simply for what is.

You Are the Unreliable Witness

We cannot trust the evidence of our memory, or even our eyes, because our personal histories and social conditioning mean we can never be objective on life. Given our propensity to accept the authority and world-views that are imposed on us in these ways, even the subtlest things can influence us.

The psychologist Elizabeth Loftus showed 150 people a film of a car accident and then divided them into two groups, each of which was asked questions about what they'd seen. The only difference was that one group was given a trick question—"How fast was the car going when it passed the barn?" There was no barn in the film.

A week later, both groups were given a recall test and asked if they had seen a barn. Among those who got the trick question, 17 percent said yes, compared to less than 3 percent of the group who weren't originally asked about the barn. For almost one in five people, a nonexistent barn had been added to their memories—due to a subtlety in wording, and because Elizabeth was a scientist and therefore had a degree of perceived authority over them.[4]

She showed another film of a car accident, and this time asked her participants to estimate the speed at which the cars were traveling, using the question "How fast were the cars going when they . . ." The next words were either *smashed into, connected with, collided with, bumped into,* or *hit,* each other. Everyone saw the same film, but their answers varied according to the words used. When *smashed* was used, the speed was estimated at 41mph; when *connected* was used, the speed was 31mph, a difference of about 25 percent. A week later she asked the same people if there was any broken glass at the scene of the accident. There wasn't—but 32 percent of the people said there was, when the word *smashed* had been used in their original question, compared with 14 percent when the word *hit* was used. That's more than double.

We carve out reality so it makes sense to us and fits the life we are used to. In fact, this *is* reality. The stories of our lives *are* our lives.

Turn back a few pages now, and look at the heading again, the one that says, "Can you believe the evidence of your own eyes?" Look particularly at the fifth word: *evividence*. There is no such word; but did you read it as *evidence*, the first time around? You did so because that was the word you were expecting; because we are taught to read the flavor or mood of things rather than their actual content. In this way we project what we "know" onto the world (even if we actually "know" nothing).

There is a story that when Columbus first arrived in America, the natives he met on the shoreline saw him as a god because he seemed to materialize before their eyes. Their culture did not have big ships, only canoes, and so they literally did not see his armada on the horizon, because they had no reference for it. There is another story that tells of what happened when the deep-jungle-dwelling tribes of Africa stepped out onto the plains for the first time: they believed that the animals they saw around them in the distance were actually very close and very tiny. Before they left their canopy of trees, they had no concept of long distances, having lived their whole lives surrounded closely by plants and foliage, in a vertical, not a horizontal world.

Such psychological tricks are the basis of the Ninja arts of deception—we all see what we expect to see. What the Ninja also knew is that there is no absolute truth—about you, the world, who you are "supposed" to be, the things you can do or what you must fail at—no matter what you have been told or learned from life. All of it is a matter of perspective, and "truth" is whatever you believe it to be. This gives you a remarkable opportunity for freedom if you are prepared to take it.

Mastery of Magus energy is about developing a skillful mind; one able to make magic by conjuring a new world from the ashes of accepted truth. A first step in this is to empty the mind of indoctrinated beliefs and accept that we just don't have solid answers to many of life's questions. This is a challenge for us in the West, since our culture is involved almost to obsession in training the mind to look at life in a particular way, where everything is known and ordered. We are taught that we should have an opinion on everything, even if we have the answer to nothing, and that these opinions will serve us for life. Reality is far more Zen than this.

There is a story that Chuang Tzu and his friend were walking by a riverbank one day. "The fish are really enjoying themselves in the water!" said Chuang Tzu.

"You are not a fish," his surly friend replied. "How do you know they are enjoying themselves?"

"Ah, but you are not me," said Chuang Tzu. "How do you know I don't know the fish are enjoying themselves?!"

Chuang Tzu's friend is caught in the tricks of the mind, which thinks it has an answer to everything. The truth, however, is that not much can really be known because there is always another perspective on everything.* These tricks of the mind can hold us fixed in a worldview that does not serve us at all if we don't remain fluid and open to change. But there is a spiritual opportunity here if we are prepared to look at things in a different way. As the singer-songwriter Damien Rice puts it: "It's not hard to grow when you know that you just don't know."

Jeff was a workshop participant who asked to speak to me after class one day. He wanted to tell me about his life. His father had been violent and abusive toward him, his sister, and his mother, and Jeff had spent his early years fending off attacks or listening to his mother and sister crying as dad turned his attention to them.

When Jeff reached age seventeen he could take it no longer. His father returned home drunk one night and began to attack him and his sister. When Jeff was thrown over a desk he picked up the first thing his hand landed on: a paperknife. He turned around and stabbed his father with it.

His father survived and had Jeff arrested for this "unprovoked attack." All charges were dropped, however, when the circumstances of the case were heard. But that was enough for Jeff. He left home and

---

*I sometimes pose paradoxical or Zen-like questions to my students, the purpose being that while the rational mind is occupied with pondering the imponderable, we can gain useful insights through our more intuitive senses. One of my favorite questions (which actually does have an answer) is this one: Is infinity an odd or an even number? See if you can find the solution. If you can, try this: What is the lowest possible number that infinity can therefore be?

didn't see his father again for thirty years. He would never have seen him again, except for a phone call from his sister one day to tell him their father was dying. Jeff decided to make peace with the man who had made his life so unbearable and drove 600 miles to see him. His father denied everything, however, and, in fact, accused Jeff of making it up.

It is hard to forgive anyone who can't even acknowledge there is something to forgive. It is even harder to overcome thirty years of pain. But Jeff managed it. He stayed by his father's side, tending to his needs until his father died. He then handled the funeral arrangements, ensuring to the last detail that his father's wishes were met.

What Jeff wanted to know, after he'd told me this story, is how he could get through the barriers of fear and the feelings of powerlessness he had been left with as a result of his early years. He was experiencing problems with his marriage and difficulties with his children, which he recognized as related to his upbringing, and he didn't know what to do anymore.

"You're asking the wrong person, Jeff," I said. "I don't see an ounce of fear or powerlessness in you. In fact, you're one of the bravest people I've met. You did right by your father, despite all that he did to you, and you will do right by your children. You don't have it in you to do otherwise."

Jeff's face brightened. The thing was that Jeff was already in his power, which was evident from his actions toward his father and his calmness and humility in relating his story to me. He just couldn't see it, because there was still a part of him that had bought in to his father's description of the world. Once he could see a different "truth," though, he could free himself from confusion and his self-limitations could begin to melt away. He returned to his family with a new commitment to resolve his problems. Clarity was the key to Jeff's future so he could step into Magus energy.

What-Ifs and Limiting Beliefs

Anything is one of a million paths.

—DON JUAN

The enemies to clarity are the *what-ifs* of the mind. Self-doubt. "What if my father was right all along?" "I know I'm not happy, but what happens if I change things?" "What if I quit my job—how will my family survive?"

What-ifs are self-limiting beliefs, temptations to fall back into habit and the opinions of others because the alternative seems too daunting: if we believe there is something other than who we are, we must concede that we have spent at least some of our lives being who we are not. We must then break with these habits of our lifetimes and step out of our comfort zones of false identity to discover who we really are. Reinventing ourselves seems like the biggest thing in the world.

If we can do so, however, and embrace our potential for change, then, like Jeff, we are on our way to Magus energy. The opportunity to reinvent ourselves means we can, at last, start living our own truths. As Noam Chomsky wrote: "If you assume that there is an instinct for freedom, that there are opportunities to change things, there's a chance you may contribute to making a better world. [But] that's *your* choice."[5]

The questions these what-ifs raise are important and demand answers. But they do need to be answered and not dwelt upon, or we will find ourselves stuck in a place of bewilderment and, ultimately, of inaction. There is some guidance in the Ninja traditions for correct decision making: we need to think skillfully so we can make effective choices. In modern terms, all this may really require is paper and a pen.

We often confuse desire with action. We want something so we almost expect it to magically materialize or someone else to provide it. But wanting a thing will not make it appear; getting it requires that we put our energy into it and make a movement toward it. This is more easily seen if we simply make five columns on the paper, headed as follows.

Situation	Desire	Action	Outcome	Consequences
What is not working for me?	What do I want instead? (What needs to change?)	What will I do to get it?	What will change when I get what I want?	How will I deal with these changes?

Use these columns to help you see what needs to change and how to go about it. Getting it down on paper will make it clearer and show you the necessary steps.

The most important columns are the last three. Once you have listed what you want, make a note in column three of the things you need to do—because it is actions, not dreams, that change things. You may need to take a number of them to reach your goal, but they are often very simple, practical things you just haven't seen before. For example, one man I worked with felt he was letting down his family, because he would often make promises that he'd be home at a certain time so they could all do something together, but invariably he would arrive late and the family's plans would be ruined. This was leading to arguments and just wasn't a behavior that was working for him. What he wanted was to keep his promises, and not doing so was tearing him up.

When he made his list, he saw that what he needed was to negotiate time more effectively with his family. Rather than saying he'd be home "around 7:30" (which set up an expectation but still got him off the hook of actually being there on time, since 8:00 or even 8:30 is also "around" 7:30), he began to be more precise with his words. The other thing he needed to do was simplicity itself: Buy a watch! He had never owned a watch, so he never knew what time it was. Making agreements based on timekeeping would therefore always lead to conflict, as he had little hope of keeping his word. His first practical action was to get one.

Column four and column five are there for you to list the consequences of your actions and identify the risks you are taking. You can then see what the real outcomes might be and identify ways of dealing with them (or, indeed, decide the outcomes are not worth it) instead of allowing what-ifs and fantasies to rule your thinking.

Finally, if things do not go exactly according to plan, don't fall into the trap of believing you made a *mistake*. When something veers off plan, it is not a mistake, it is an inspiration in itself, an opportunity for further learning and growth, and for the Magus to use her magic to make something even better appear. Do not define these off-plan adventures as *failures*. Calmly and objectively go back to your column headings instead, and make another list of what now needs to change. Then repeat the process as before.

To engage with the world of the Magus, we also need to know what our real ambitions are—the ones that underlie our conditioned selves—so we can then hope to meet them. The initiatory task of the Magus is to find vision in life, based on something authentic that has the ring of truth to it. We can learn more about our true motivations and visions by interviewing the soul.

EXERCISE 16

Konpaku: *Meeting Your Soul-Self*

Close your eyes and breathe into your heart (the place of desire). See in your mind's eye that, beyond all the labels and opinions, and beyond the material world, there is a part of you that is pure consciousness. This is *konpaku*—what the Ninja might understand as soul or spirit.

Stage 1: Intention

See yourself as this spiritual essence at a time before you were even conceived, a time when you were still part of the pool of conscious energy that suffuses the universe. Explore that feeling of connection for a while.

What does it feel like to be you at this time? What did you know then—before life got in the way of this pure knowledge? What have you forgotten about yourself that you remember now?

Now see yourself moving forward in time to the moment when your spirit-self made a choice to leave this universal pool and take human form. You had a reason for this, an intention. This was your soul mission, your true purpose in being.

What was this reason? What did you come here to do, and what gifts and abilities did you bring with you for achieving this?

What burdens or handicaps did you also set yourself up to overcome so this trip here would never be dull and you could learn something from it?

What do you still have to learn?

When you have your answers, breathe out, and open your eyes.

Stage 2: Re-membering

Now make three notes to yourself:

1. The reason I am here and my true mission is . . .
2. The gifts and abilities that will help me achieve this are . . .
3. The challenges I gave myself are . . .

Stage 3: Your Mantra of Commitment

With your eyes closed again, and now breathing into your solar plexus (the place of your will and commitment), focus on the ambitions of your soul and hold onto them as you see your spirit-essence beginning its journey from energy to human form and then entering your mother's womb.

Repeat to yourself: "I remain committed to my purpose."

See yourself growing in the womb and repeat those same words again. Now see yourself being born and repeat the same mantra, this time out loud.

Move forward in time and see yourself at age one, five, ten, twenty . . . right up to your current age. Repeat your commitment out loud at every stage. If there is a body movement that goes with this, a dance, a gesture, a mudra, make it every time you voice your commitment. Let your body know the energy of your intention.

When you reach your current age, make your commitment out loud three times, allowing your body to move to your words. Then open your eyes and come back to normal awareness.

Stage 4: Doing

Take a few more breaths and allow kindness to fill your heart. Kindness toward yourself, toward others who have played their role in your life and the mission of your soul, kindness even toward your enemies, for without them you would not be the person you are now, doing this exercise in a place where you can make a choice about your future.

Now begin to write again, in a stream of consciousness, reflecting on the mood rather than the detail of the mission you have just experienced, and in answer to this question:

What, on Earth, do I most need to do to be true to my reason for being?

Don't veto anything, just write until you feel like stopping. Then read what you have written and make a list, as you go through it, of all your ambitions that remain unfulfilled. Add a date next to each one by which you will have completed it. It doesn't matter if some of these things take a day and others take ten years; you will never get them done at all unless you begin them sometime. That time is now.

It is action, not wishful thinking or half-made commitments that change things in our lives. In the words of don Juan: "The way to live—the path with heart—is not introspection but presence in the world. This world is the warrior's hunting ground."[6] Make it your hunting ground too. Begin the process of honoring your mission by taking one action immediately that moves you closer to your vision. Make a phone call, write a letter, do whatever needs to be done to get things moving. Don't even think about it, just do it.

NINE

The Initiation of the Magus: Letting Go of Confusion

Techniques of Clarity

It's the weirdest thing. I feel like I've been in a coma for about twenty years and I'm just waking up.

—KEVIN SPACEY IN THE FILM *AMERICAN BEAUTY*

The quest for vision is a make-or-break point for many on the warrior path. You may not have noticed much difference in the reactions of people around you—or perhaps they praised you—when you took on your fears and overcame them, or when you reclaimed your power and discovered new strengths, self-awareness, self-direction, and integrity. Magus energy is a whole different ball game though.

When you tap into the Magus, you are required by the journey itself to question everything. This means your relationships, job, past, present, future—who you really are. This test of initiation can be unnerving for you, but it can be terrifying for those closest to you because they will see you changing and, for one thing, will realize they can change too. Freedom is the scariest thing in the world for some people, those who are more comfortable with rules and known routines, even if they make no sense or act to their detriment. When you start behaving differently in the face of this convention, their response may well be to try to hold you back by informing you once again of your limitations instead of supporting your vision of a limitless future. As Lyndon B. Johnson humorously put it, "If one morning I walked on top of the water across the Potomac River, the headline that afternoon would read 'President Can't Swim.'"

You also have responsibilities and a duty of care to the people you have allowed into your life so far. You cannot just become someone else overnight; you still have to be there for them. You are now between a rock and a hard place. Welcome. Pull up a chair.

How you deal with this is one of the questions that faces every Magus, and there are no textbook answers. All you can do is trust that the universe means you no harm, that there is a *musuhi*—a creative and harmonizing power—that is working in your best interests. You have to accept a leap of faith.

For the Ninja, personal freedom and personal integrity were two of the most important human qualities when facing this world of faith. They understood that choice determined everything and, while they could not always know the agenda of the gods, they could act with impeccability and authenticity in their own decisions. This exercise will help you explore the choices that may also face you.

EXERCISE 17

The Two Roads

Close your eyes, breathe deeply a few times, and relax. Without forcing anything, allow an image to form in your mind of a road you are walking down. This road is your life, and with each step you walk further into your future—tomorrow, next week, next month, ten, twenty, thirty, forty, fifty years from now.

How does this road look to you? Who else (if anyone) is on this path? What is going on around you? How do you feel?

At a certain point, you arrive at a place where the road forks and you must decide to walk down one path or the other. Choose one now and walk it, knowing that this one is the road you will travel if you decide to turn your back on your soul mission and the promise you made to yourself to live fully and heroically when you chose to be born to this world.

How does this road look to you? Who is here with you? How do you feel now?

Keep walking and eventually you will meet another person on this path. It is as if he or she is expecting you. Looking closer, you realize why. This person is *you,* the you at the end of this inauthentic life, when there are no further choices available; it is the you who can look back over your life and see how you have lived.

How does this person look? Is there anyone else there or is the person alone?

Speak with this older you, and ask questions: *How do you feel about yourself, about this life you have lived, about the choices and decisions you have made? Is there anything you would have done differently or are you happy with the way things turned out?*

Ask the person for one piece of advice, from your older to your younger self. *What suggestions does he or she have for you about the future that is still available to you?*

Thank the person for this information and, knowing you can return for further counsel at any time, turn around and begin to retrace your steps.

As you do so, the older you hands you a piece of paper on which are written some words you can't quite make out yet. Put this in your pocket and return to the fork in the road.

Open your eyes and record your observations.

Close your eyes again and return to the road. Now you have time to study the message you have been given so take it out of your pocket and unfold it. The heading on the paper is one word: *Obituary,* and, beneath it, is your name.

As you read what is written you are aware that these are the words of someone who loved you very much and knew you well. The obituary is a kindly summation of your life by someone who knows, nonetheless, that you did not live your promise or remain true to your soul.

What does your obituary tell you about your life? What were your major achievements—and failings? Were you happy, free, fulfilled?

Open your eyes and write down what this obituary says.

Now forget this information for the time being. Close your eyes again and relax. You stand at the same fork in the road. This time, take the other path, the road of authenticity, the path you will walk if you live the mission of your soul.

How does this road look? Who is here with you? How do you feel?

Eventually you will meet another person on this road: the *you* at the end of *this* life. *How does this person look? How does he or she seem? How does this you feel about himself or herself and the choices he or she made? Is this person happy with the way things turned out or would he or she have done things differently?*

Again, ask for one piece of advice, from the older to the younger you. *What does he or she tell you?*

Record your observations.

Closing your eyes again, you are given another piece of paper, and this time you know what to expect. Turn and retrace your steps, back to the fork in the road, and read what is written there, the obituary of someone who lived his or her promise and was true to his or her soul. *What do these words tell you about your authentic life?*

Bring yourself back to normal awareness now. Open your eyes and write down what this obituary says.

People who complete this exercise invariably find that an authentic life, a life lived true to their vision, is brighter, more colorful, happier, more exciting, and more fulfilling, no matter what difficulties they may face on their journey to authenticity. One workshop participant, Dru, put it this way: "The coward and the hero are both afraid of what lies ahead; it's what they choose that separates them. The coward runs but the hero has the courage and discipline to go through what he must. This is what makes him a hero—the possibility of fighting for his life."

If this is the same for you, take the obituary you have written for your inauthentic self and burn it, then scatter its ashes to the four winds—the Godai element of Air, domain of the Magus—so you are free to commit to something new and better. Keep the obituary for your authentic self in a place where you can see it always.

Breaking Out of Habit

Warriors know the importance of shedding our skins—breaking mental habits and getting rid of the armor of the past if we are to live a vibrant life instead of one based on old, outdated, irrelevant decisions (some not even made by us). The Ninja knew this as *karumijutsu*—the art of lightening the body—a technique that used the power of Air (breathwork) to let go of illusions. (See "Air Breathing," later on in the chapter.) We must do what makes sense for us *now,* in this weird world without truth, not repeat the things we have grown used to, if we are to be present, to evolve, and to stay conscious in this life.

Our minds make us creatures of habit, and the more we give our energy over to the maintenance of these, the less we actually engage with the world or act with full awareness. Life becomes like driving a route we are used to and then "waking up" thirty miles later as we get out of the car, wondering where that last forty-five minutes went to. We limit ourselves to the 5 percent of our brains that we use to get by, while feeding the routine with 95 percent of our energy. That is not a good return in anyone's book: 95 percent of our energy expended on 5 percent awareness and engagement with life. And yet most of us do it every day.

Breaking these habits can change the whole dynamic of a life. Breaking habits involves us in the process of living our vision, instead of bouncing like a pinball off the situations presented to us or stumbling unconsciously through the day. We must be present in every unique moment of our life if we want to experience it for what it is.

EXERCISE 18
Breaking Habits

When we break habits, we stay alert and we free our minds, which is the work of the Magus and the initiation of the West. We then have greater capacity for mental flexibility.

You can begin the process now by doing something as "radical" and "unique" as getting out of bed on the other side tomorrow! Or set your alarm clock for a different time. In fact, one of the simplest and surprisingly effective things we can all do is to take off our watches. We then have to engage with the day, watching the sun in the sky and the movements of others in order to gauge the time. Just for tomorrow, spend the day without a watch as your first gesture of breaking routine.

If you are really inspired by the warrior way, then think about the thing you would *least* like to do—and do that. Perhaps it is jumping from a plane, perhaps it is telling your partner you love her. And perhaps if you do this, you will receive a jolt of understanding as to why this thing unnerves you. Then you will have found a new route into yourself and a deepening of your clarity about who you are and what is important to you.

It is amazing how simple things can lead to dramatic change. A workshop participant once told me how he decided to do something "radical" and "change his life." His "amazing departure from routine" was to take a different bus route to work one morning. He was joking as he told me this, but the fact was it *did* change his life. It was on this bus that he met his future wife, someone he would never have encountered if he'd caught the number 14 as usual. Perhaps there are no coincidences, just synchronicities and meetings waiting to happen. But how will we know unless we make ourselves available to them?

Making a Refusal

I followed all the rules—man and god's—you followed none of them. And they all loved you more.
—A character in the film *Legends of the Fall*

One habit we are all good at is leaving our business unfinished. It is often what we don't say or do that defines our relationships with the world. When we leave things undone or unsaid through neglect (or done and said but not corrected when they could and should have been), they add to our repertoire of regrets and keep us hooked in one place, one from which it is harder to achieve our visions.

EXERCISE 19
The Hooks of the Past

Close your eyes and breathe into a place at the top of your neck, where your spine meets your skull. This is the hindbrain, the oldest part of the brain, which we once relied on exclusively, thousands of years ago, when we were all utterly connected to life. The hindbrain knows that we are part of everything. Breathe into this place, take your awareness to it, and sit with it for a few minutes.

Stage 1: Hooks and Themes

Do not force anything, but allow yourself to be gently informed by this part of your mind as you play with this question: *When I look back at my life and relationships with others, what common theme starts to emerge?* Sum it up in one word if you can.

The themes that run through our lives can be aspects of our soul mission. If you constantly find yourself in situations where commitment is an issue, for example, and this is the word that comes to mind for you, then this is a part of your reason for being. The problems you have had concerning commitment—in your relationships, decisions, and dreams—are learning and breakthrough opportunities you have provided for yourself. Now that you are aware of them you can use this information to keep yourself on track for the future. As you do so you will be practicing the Ninja art of *nukewaza* (escape from old programs).*

Open your eyes when you are ready.

Stage 2: Old Photographs

To double check that you have correctly identified a key theme of your life, find a photograph of yourself from before the age of five and look into your eyes. What do you see there?

Michael brought a photograph to one of our therapy sessions, an old black and white image of himself taken in the 1960s, a very young boy sitting in a garden, frowning at the camera, while a young girlfriend sat next to him, leaning adoringly on his arm. It illustrated every relationship Michael had ever had with a girl, including his current one—she wanting to be closer to him while he pushed her away. For Michael, "emotional distance" was one of the themes of his life and a hook that held him to the past so he could not embrace the future he really wanted. Now that he saw this, he began to create opportunities for loving closeness. One of his first gestures was to book a romantic weekend for himself and his girlfriend. Twelve months on now, they are married.

Of course, Michael still has fears about intimacy and commitment, but now they are conscious, so he can refuse them when they arise and stay true to his vision of a future where love is possible.

Stage 3: Thanking Your Co-Creators

There is a final part to this exercise—if you want to take it. Many of the people you have drawn into your life will have presented you with

---

Nukewaza normally refers to physical techniques for escape from body holds and locks, but we are equally held by our minds and, in fact, since thought determines action, the tyranny of the mind can often be harder for us to escape from.

examples of this theme. Your lovers, friends, even your enemies, are all co-creators of your present. They are your guides and mentors, if you choose to see things this way, because without them, you would not be you. These people share the same issue or life theme with you. That is why you were drawn to each other.

As a gesture to honor this, write down the word that signifies a key theme in your life (which is theirs too) and send it to them. Do it anonymously so they have the freedom to do with it as they wish. Don't allow yourself to become attached to any particular outcome, either. Just notice how the world changes, for them and for you.

Burning from the Inside—Impeccability: *Giri* and *Bushido*

The Warrior's Code of Vision

Castaneda pointed out the power of impeccability when he spoke of a quarrel he once had with his teacher, don Juan, in the middle of a desert. Castaneda took himself away to sulk, thinking don Juan would soon come over to sort out his problems. Don Juan, however, just sat quietly, hour after hour, as Castaneda wallowed in gloom some feet away. "I finally realized that this man was not like my father, who could make twenty New Year's resolutions and cancel them all," said Castaneda. "Don Juan's decisions were irrevocable as far as he was concerned. They could be canceled out only by other decisions."[1]

Eventually, Castaneda relented and made his peace with don Juan, having learned something important from this event: that don Juan didn't have to be there at all. He could have got up and walked away from his student at any time; he did not have to sit in that desert heat staring at nothing all day while his student dealt with the issues that had created their disagreement. It was impeccability that kept don Juan in that desert. He had made a commitment to his student and himself that he would be present in their relationship and true to it during their time together. This level of impeccability is what we must all strive for— because without a commitment to something, we are nothing.

Impeccability is what the Ninja knew as giri. It is a sense of duty and personal discipline, which begins with self-awareness and honesty. You make a commitment and you stick to it, no matter what. It is this drive that gets things done. Impeccability is the warrior's "burning from the inside" as she commits her vision to action.

We all need a vision for our lives, something that will take us into a better future. *Bushido* is the code of the warrior, her guideline for living.* It expresses her intention to believe in the things that have meaning to her, knowing it is this alone that creates her truth in the world. Underlying it all is the intention to love life. This is clarity, the understanding that we make our reality through conscious choice and find direction for ourselves by actively deciding how we will live.

The following is an extract from the bushido of a fourteenth-century warrior:

> *I have no parents; I make the heavens and earth my parents*
> *I have no home; I make awareness my home*
> *I have no life or death; I make the tides of breathing my life*
>   *and death*
> *I have no divine power; I make honesty my divine power*
> *I have no means; I make understanding my means . . .*
> *I have no strategy; I make "unshadowed by thought" my*
>   *strategy*
> *I have no designs; I make "seizing opportunity" my design*
> *I have no miracles; I make "right action" my miracles*
> *I have no principles; I make adaptability to all circumstances*
>   *my principles . . .*
> *I have no talents; I make wit my talent*
> *I have no friends; I make my mind my friend*
> *I have no enemy; I make carelessness my enemy*
> *I have no sword; I make absence of self my sword . . .* [2]

---

*The term *bushido* comes from the Samurai schools but was absorbed into Ninja philosophy through contact with disaffected or disenfranchised Samurai warriors who joined Ninja clans over the years.

Bushido is both a refusal and an affirmation. The first part of every statement is the warrior's refusal to accept social definitions of who he is, what he must have, or how he must behave; the second part is his conscious commitment to his own vision. Underlying it is self-determination, self-reliance, and self-belief. The warrior is determined to think and act for himself and, once the code is written, he will never be swayed from it unless by another conscious decision on his part. This is the nature of impeccability.

Writing a bushido as an enduring framework for your own vision is one of the most powerful exercises for remembering who you are and giving yourself a guide to *right action*. It is commitment on a grand scale, and not something to be taken lightly because, once written, it must be followed impeccably and can only be reversed by further soul-searching and another fully conscious decision to make a change to your life. If you are ready for this, here is a method for writing your bushido.

EXERCISE 20
Making Bushido

When he was working with very depressed patients, the psychoanalyst Viktor Frankl would sometimes bluntly ask them, "Why do you not kill yourself?" Facing this question head-on, his patients realized that there was always something to live for—their children, a love of opera, a good book; whatever it was that most mattered to them. Once they acknowledged this, his patients understood that there *was* a reason and meaning to their lives and that they *did* have a vision for the future, no matter how unrefined. This was often the first step toward their cure.

In fact, the opposite could also have been asked, as the Ninja more likely did: "What would I die to protect?" This is the first step in the creation of bushido—bringing into awareness the things that are important to us so we can see the meaning in our lives. To make bushido, begin by listing the things that matter to you—those things, values, or people without whom your life would be less rich.

What do I truly believe in?
What do I live for?
What would I die to defend?

Dream on it for a while before you commit your words to paper. No one else need ever see this list (and it is not for anyone else anyway), so be totally honest with yourself and don't veto anything that is important. These things are all you.

Now take your list and paint a picture or write a poem that symbolizes and summarizes these things as a personal bushido—your own code for living—like the one above. Let yourself go and see what you create.

The poet John Keats wrote that

Beauty is truth, truth beauty—that is all
Ye know on earth, and all ye need to know.

This may indeed be all there is to life: that which is beautiful moves us, and gives us meaning, *is* the truth; the only truth we need. Once we commit to that, we have understood the energy of the Magus.

Air: The Third Ally

Air (fu) is our ally within the Godai for stilling the mind so we can see through illusion and find our clarity. Take yourself to a place of beauty in nature where you can feel the breeze on your skin and see the wind in the trees. Watch as the leaves dance, going with the flow of the air. Allow your body to move gently to the rhythm of these leaves and your mind to empty. It is as if you *are* the wind, free to move at will, as quickly or as slowly as you wish. There is no need to dance with any particular truth or to limit yourself in any way. You are held by your own bushido, your chosen way of life.

For the Ninja, Air represents the highest of freedoms. It is reflected in "feelings of wisdom and benevolence, and in conscious consideration of one's interactions with others."[3] Fill your mind with images of the things and people you love and allow the wind to send your blessings to them, a kiss of unconditional love carried on the invisible breeze, from your heart to theirs. These people and things *are* your bushido, your vision. They are what is truly important.

Our purpose in life as conscious human beings is to build good memories, so that when death taps us on the shoulder we can look back on a life well lived. Make it part of your agenda to do something to create one good memory for yourself and one other person, just for today. But do it every day.

Hira No Kamae: Air Movement

The Ninja body movement that reflects the freedom of Air is *hira no kamae*. You begin with your legs apart slightly wider than hip width, knees softly bent. Your arms are stretched out at your sides, shoulder height, with elbows soft and palms up, as your body faces your imaginary adversary (the illusions of mind that have been holding you fixed in the habit of "truth" instead of vision).

Your opponent moves toward you and you react, not with force, but by gently circling out of the way. Simply spin 180 degrees on your left foot, lifting your right and bringing it back down so you are facing in the opposite direction. Your adversary rushes harmlessly past you, just as you refuse to become trapped in limiting beliefs. Allow yourself to feel love for this adversary as you breathe out and let old patterns go. This enemy and these patterns have been important to your learning and survival so far, which is why they are worthy of love. But now is the time to release them.

Air Breathing *(Karumijutsu)*

Air moves in a circular way and on most days is measured and gentle. Reflect this movement in your mind, allowing whatever thoughts to arise as they will but without attachment to them. As you do so, breathe in through your nose for a count of seven and out through your mouth for a count of eleven.

When you have this breathing pattern established, take your attention to your brow and breathe into your "third eye." With every breath, you feel your connection to the universe grow until you are charged with crystal radiance. Repeat to yourself: *I see with total clarity the reality of things, and I embrace the vision of my life.* Know that you do.

Everything can be taken from a man but one thing: the last of the human freedoms—to choose one's attitude in any given set of circumstances, to choose one's own way . . .
— VIKTOR FRANKL

WARRIOR COMMITMENT

I Free My Mind and Become the Magus

With the gentleness of a summer breeze, I open myself to vision and let go of habitual thoughts and patterns of living.

My bushido is my guide. These are all the rules I need. I act with impeccability toward those people and things I love and, through this commitment, I allow love to materialize and grow stronger in my life.

I choose not to waste energy on things that do not serve me or those I love. Freedom and happiness become my outlook and I accept responsibility for ensuring that these things are reflected in the way I live.

I make this commitment to myself with full consciousness and as a gesture of clarity, to honor myself, as a mark of self-respect, right thinking, and right action.

I let this commitment go to the universe, while allowing its energy to guide and support me, and I believe and trust that things will be this way.

SIGNED: _____

DATE: _____

knowing the earth

The woods are lovely, dark and deep,
But I have promises to keep,
And miles to go before I sleep,
And miles to go before I sleep.

—ROBERT FROST

The trees in the distance were beginning to fill with snow, silhouetting them in white against the darkening forest sky as I threw the last shovel of earth on top of the young woman lying in her shallow grave. It was the night before Christmas Eve. The ground was hard and the night was cold, but the woods were lovely . . .

This young woman, my client, Kathy, came to see me during a depression that had lasted months. She couldn't eat or sleep. She was tired of life. There is a healing practice I sometimes use in cases such as these. It is called the Burial of the Warrior.

Depression is a form of fatigue with life. Our energy is depleted because we are constantly up against ourselves and dwelling on who we have been, not who we are in this unique moment that heralds our freedom. The things that depress us are arisings of the mind, a form of unskillful thinking where we believe that "the world out there" is right about us, when actually there is no world "out there" and nothing to be right about. We have to get around the conditioned mind if we are to overcome our illusions and be healthy and free. That is the purpose of the burial. Something happens when people are buried in this way: they gather strength from the Earth and find a new zest for living.

There is a rich spiritual history associated with voluntary burials. The Ninja knew of them and incorporated them into their stealth training. The tradition was also known in India, where Mima O spent some part of his life. Here, fakirs, sadhus, and holy men would slow

150

their breathing, go into trance, and entomb themselves alive. One of them, Ramaswamy, claimed to have been buried for one hundred years when his tomb was discovered in Amritsar, India, and he was set free. Ramaswamy was questioned by scientists and scholars and gave accurate accounts of events of the day—from a century before he was found. Did he really sit there in quiet meditation for one hundred years? Who knows?

Kathy was to be buried for twelve hours to face her own "dark night of the soul." Not quite one hundred years, but long enough in darkness, underground, with no sights or sounds from the outside world.

With her internment complete, I sat down to keep vigil over her, and looked up at the clear night sky. A shooting star crossed the horizon—Kathy's soul searching for peace, perhaps.

The night passed slowly, and it was cold.

Then, in the morning, something remarkable happened: before her twelve hours were up Kathy asked to be released, to rejoin the play of life. "I feel so much better, lighter, alive!" she said.

As we walked out of the woods, we were amazed to see that the fields around us were covered in snow; yet none of it had fallen at our burial site. How is it possible that snow can avoid a certain spot? And yet there was not even a dusting of frost near us, just a circle of clear forest floor for thirty feet around the place where Kathy had dug her grave.

All the way back, Kathy marveled at the wonder of the dawn, the brightness of the day, the beauty of the leafless trees against the blue-white winter sky. Being with her was like reliving those childhood Christmases where magic sparkles around you and eyes open wide in wonder. Kathy was back with us, alive and in love with life.

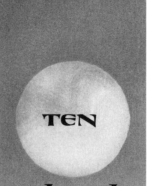

TEN

Chi (Earth): The Soul Warrior's Fatigue

Avoiding the Wide Arms of Sleep

Let yourself go with the disease, be with it, keep company with it—this is the way to be rid of it.

—Bruce Lee

There may come a time for all of us when we grow tired of life; when the demands, problems, power trips, and games become too much for us and life loses meaning. If you have experienced this feeling, you can be sure you are not alone.

Viktor Frankl, the psychiatrist I mentioned earlier, writes of a survey among European students that found that 25 percent showed a marked degree of "existential vacuum" (i.e., lack of meaning in their lives). Among Americans it was 60 percent.

"The existential vacuum manifests mainly in a state of boredom [which is] now causing, and certainly bringing to psychiatrists, more problems to solve than distress," Frankl writes. "Let us consider, for instance, 'Sunday neurosis,' that kind of depression which afflicts people who become aware of the lack of content in their lives when the rush of the busy week is over and the void within themselves becomes manifest. Not a few cases of suicide can be traced back to this."[1]

For the Ninja, this loss of meaning was one form of *kuro* (suffering), which we might also call soul fatigue. It is the battle between the spirit, with its desire to go on to fulfill the mission our souls have set, and the emotions, often bruised by life. It is the temptation to give in and settle for the dull and sterile view we have been taught to have of the world—the image of a fear-filled place built on separation and anxiety—or, in extreme cases, to give up on life entirely. Overcoming this fatigue is the initiatory challenge of the Soul Warrior, the man or woman who is seeking the laughter and silence of mature spirituality and wisdom.

The aim of the Soul Warrior is to rediscover the balance and connection he first knew as a child, so he can use his earned skills of courage, power, and clarity with a real and continued zest for living. If he can do so, he will find more than just warrior energy waiting for him, for this is also his final test and, if he passes it, all gateways will be open to him and he can finally move through them into the Void, the original bliss of connection we all felt as newborns.

In order to do so, however, the Soul Warrior will have to face his shadow: the fatigued Cynic who wants to escape into the fantasy of a life beyond his control, where all things are accounted for and he can only accept them. A person on the Soul Warrior path can give in to this sense of boredom, resignation, ennui, or depression at life's struggles, or he can embrace his fatigue as an ally in the understanding that every time we are tired of life, we have a chance to look more closely at who this person is that is tired and what changes he needs to make to feel better and more enlivened. The message from fatigue, in fact, is: keep going because you are about to enter a time of major breakthrough and life change.

The Meaning in Suffering

There is an alchemy in sorrow. It can be transmuted into wisdom.

—Pearl Buck

Ninja believe that if there is meaning in life, there must also be meaning in suffering, for sorrow, pain, grief, and fatigue are also a part of life. Our tendency may be to push our pains away, to sublimate or ignore them, and to let our sorrows drown. The problem is that sorrows are excellent swimmers and they will continue to resurface unless we acknowledge and deal with them. One strategy for the warrior is to use his suffering to advantage by living it fully and learning from it so that fatigue becomes an ally, not an enemy.

There are many ways to use our suffering positively. One is simply to accept our pains with dignity instead of concealing them, ignoring them, running from them, or wishing for something else. If we can do that we will not lose sight of who we are but, rather, come to see our suffering as simply a part of being human. We can then get on with our lives, knowing that we control fatigue, it does not control us. When we acknowledge our pain we can deal with it; while it remains unconscious, we will operate forever from an inner place of sorrow and so remain slaves to the fates.

In my twenties, I knew a woman named Sophie, one of the most beautiful, carefree, intelligent, charming, and humorous people I have ever met. Everyone loved Sophie, and every man wanted to date her. By all the "normal" standards of the time (the early 1980s) this might have been thought strange, because Sophie was an amputee, and society had a different norm at that time in its response to the "disabled."

Sophie lost her leg in a motorcycle accident at the age of nineteen. For many people, this would have been enough to throw them into despair. Sophie, however, accepted her fate with dignity. She never tried to hide her disability or ask for special treatment, and this integrity as well as the beauty of her spirit is what attracted people to her. She was, in her own quiet way, an inspiration to others because she used her loss to inform her of what was important in life—quite simply, living it—and those around her absorbed her enthusiasm just by being in her presence. Sophie had lost her leg but she never lost her self.

Nowadays, Heather Mills, also an amputee, is a role model for millions as a United Nations Goodwill Ambassador and a counselor to others who have lost limbs. She was nominated for a Nobel Prize for her work in 1996. As a former model whose livelihood depended on her physical appearance, Heather could also have let tragedy rule her life; but instead, she used soul fatigue to advantage, learned from it, and channeled her energies into something worthwhile.

"Where there is sorrow, there is holy ground," as Oscar Wilde once said. As long as we are prepared to take responsibility for our lives—not in vague terms, but as the creative events we are actually living—we can learn something from our tragedies and use them to change our worlds.

We will not all lose limbs but most of us will lose something or someone important to us—a lover or a parent, a sibling, a job, a friend— at some time in our lives, and this can be devastating enough. These are times for the warrior to go within, to draw from her strengths, and to look for the underlying message in what life has sent her, so she can gain knowledge and power from it to inform and guide her life.

The way for a warrior to use fatigue to advantage is to accept it as a gift. "When a man finds that it is his destiny to suffer, he will have to accept his suffering as his task; his single and unique task. . . . No one can relieve him of his suffering or suffer in his place. His unique opportunity lies in the way in which he bears his burden."[2]

The Drawing of a Breath

Looked at more deeply, however, there is actually no suffering to be had. It is our human attachments to things, people, and expectations that lead us to believe otherwise. The natural state of the universe, meanwhile, is one of sublime non-attachment, a place where our human labels for experience do not exist in any real way.

There is a force behind all things that warriors know as the Tao. It is like the drawing of a breath. In fact, if you imagine some vast entity (the universe itself) breathing in and then out, you have just described the Tao. As it breathes out, it behaves in a way the Ninja knew as *yo* (active, vital, "masculine"); as it breathes in, it behaves in a way called *in* (receptive, calm, "feminine"). In scientific images, and in terms of "the big picture," this breathing pattern, across eons of time, is the Big

Bang that gave birth to all we know, while entropy is the drawing back in of this breath before the next Big Bang, when the cosmic life cycle will begin all over again.

If we are wise and attuned to the subtle movements of the Tao, we synchronize our breathing to it so we breathe in when it breathes out, and vice versa. Then we take in positive energy that is useful to us and, when we breathe out, we send the universe the energy most useful to it. In this way everything exists harmoniously and in balance.

If we are not so wise or get it wrong, the cycle starts to collapse and we get spun out, because, obviously, the universe has more breath (greater energy) than we do.

How we get it right is actually very simple. *We relax.* That's it. Nothing more. We stop believing that our lives are the most important things going on in the universe (we erase self-importance, in warrior terms). We refuse to get involved in trying to control every little thing that happens to us. In this way we give up our resistance to events and attachments to outcomes and avoid what we might otherwise regard as suffering.

As psychoanalyst Dina Glouberman puts it in her book, *The Joy of Burnout,*

> *When you are hopeless, give up hope.*
> *When you are humiliated, let go of pride and choose humility.*
> *When you are disillusioned, de-illusion.*
> *When you are holding on to what you know, let go and*
>   *surrender to what is about to become.*[3]

In fact, there is nothing *to* hold on to, nothing to resist or control—and nothing we really *can* control. Trying to run our lives in a rigid and inflexible way will inevitably lead to fatigue because we are putting our energy into an ultimately futile pursuit. What warriors must strive for is balance rather than control, so we are at one with the Tao instead of opposing it.

This relaxation—this letting go—is a form of actively remembering. We remember what is important: who we really are, how the world really works, and our true purpose in life, instead of battling to maintain who we *think* we are and how our lives *"should"* be.

> *The way to love anything is to realize that it might be lost.*
> —G. K. CHESTERTON

Keeping Death as Your Advisor

All human life is likened to evening dew and morning frost, considered something quite fragile and ephemeral. . . . One who is supposed to be a warrior considers it his foremost concern to keep death in mind at all times, every day and every night, from the morning of New Year's Day through the night of New Year's Eve.

> —YUZAN DAIDOJI

We are all trying to live well and enjoy our lives so we get something out of this crazy trip we are on, and have some good stories to tell and things to look back on. We have this life—let's assume it's our only life (it may well not be, but for the purpose of living it fully, the best we can say is "we don't know")—so how do we want it to end? With memories of what we could have done but didn't? Of a life led by limits that were applied to us (or which we applied to ourselves), things not said, things we didn't dare attempt or do? Or do we want a life of fun, adventure, and the stories of a hero we can tell our grandchildren, watching their eyes grow wide and their souls fill up with wonder? That's our choice.

No matter how bad life seems, or how tired of it and unhappy we sometimes are, whenever we confront fatigue, we must remember what a precious gift it is to be alive. Life gives us opportunities for experience, and through these we can change, evolve, and grow, becoming heroes to ourselves. To live consciously and fully, making the most of every opportunity life presents, we must remain calmly aware of the enduring presence of death, for this is the real incentive for us to love what we have.

Knowing we will die one day puts our lives and problems into perspective. When we know that death is near, the frantic struggle to compete and achieve seems more than futile; it seems comically ludicrous. Did we really believe that "winning" was more important than love? That we could take it all with us? That there was a point to our conflicts and disagreements beyond a simple waste of energy and precious time? Warriors see the joke, but they also recognize the seriousness, because death is ever close.

The practice of reminding themselves of their own mortality is known to warriors as Retaining Death as an Advisor. To the Ninja and Japanese Samurai it was one of the precepts of the *Ni Ten Ichi Ryu*—the Way of Warrior Strategy—awareness of death being the very thing that gives rise to more life.

The Code of the Samurai[4] tells us that when we fail to keep death in mind we become inattentive to life. When we are inattentive, we stop questioning the world and ourselves and so we fall prey to fatigue, cut off from part of our existence and stopped within the flow of time. We can always put things off, disengage from living, and decide to make a change for the better tomorrow, if we fool ourselves into thinking that we will always *have* a tomorrow. When we believe we live forever, we never really live at all, because we don't challenge life or allow it to challenge us.

With death as our advisor, we re-engage with the magic and immediacy of life so that fatigue does not overwhelm us. "The Way of the warrior *is* death," the great swordsman, Miyamoto Musashi, wrote. "It means to see things through, being resolved. . . . To die with your intention unrealized is to die uselessly. . . . [If you] consider yourself a dead body, thus becoming one with the Way of the warrior, you can pass through life with no possibility of failure."[5]

In some traditions there is a practice of moving meditation where the warrior-monk walks in graveyards and among corpses that are rotting in the open air precisely so he can reflect upon the preciousness of his ability to experience such things—*because he is alive.* He remains calm in the presence of death, knowing that it is not something to be feared, it is simply what is; something inevitable to be prepared for and a teacher to be listened to. It must inform but not concern him, because it is only by relaxing into life that he can experience its beauty and make the most of its gifts.

One of the easiest ways to work with death is therefore simply to pause, just momentarily, before taking any important decision or action, and imagine you have already died and are living your life for the second time, possibly about to repeat the same mistake. Would you still make the same decision or act in a different way?

This discipline is also a reminder that every action has consequences, some wide-ranging and long-lasting even though they might seem trivial in the present. A few moments of reflection now can save a vast amount of energy later—otherwise, unconscious decisions lead to problems that will need to be resolved and that eat further into your reserves against fatigue.

EXERCISE 21
Ankokutoshijutsu: *Deprived of Life*

Every warrior hopes that a good death will find him.
—FROM THE FILM *LEGENDS OF THE FALL*

The Ninja used a practice of sensory deprivation in their training (known as *ankokutoshijutsu*) in order to develop awareness and appreciation of the natural world. The exercise that follows is a form of ankokutoshijutsu and an adaptation of the Burial of the Warrior,* the healing practice I carried out for my client Kathy. Of course, it cannot really compare to a night spent buried in the earth, but then it is not really meant to. Rather, it is an exercise to help you appreciate how beautiful life is and

---

*We also undertake this exercise in Heart of Darkness workshops, where participants remain blindfolded for the entire five-day course, an initiatory practice of many tribal traditions. More information on darkness therapy can be found in my books, *Vodou Shaman* (Rochester,Vt.: Destiny Books, 2003) and *Darkness Visible* (Rochester, Vt.: Destiny Books, 2005). There is also an article on my Web site, www.VodouShaman.com.

how important your experiences are—all of them, no matter if they are ones of "joy" or "pain."

Stage 1: Stepping Outside of Time

Set aside a period of twelve to twenty-four hours during which you will have no contact at all with the outside world. Close your curtains, unplug your phone, TV, and stereo, turn off your lights, and tell your friends not to call. Do not eat or drink for this day either (water is okay if you need it). Simply lie still in the silent darkness, under a blanket if you wish—but do not sleep. Feel what it's like to be deprived of stimulus from the world. Allow your body to go into shutdown.

During this time, meditate on your mortality. In a gentle, not a morbid way, simply be aware that one day this dark silence is all you will have. You have a choice in how to live before that day comes.

Make a note as each hour passes of how you feel and the sensations of your body. Do you feel bored, trapped, unhappy? Or are you enjoying the experience of being alone and freefalling through time?

Stage 2: Experiencing Life

When your period of reflection is over, throw open your curtains to the dawn and go barefoot outside. Engage all your senses fully, one at a time. Look at the sky; breathe in the air and the aroma of dawn; listen to the birdsong and the laughter of children; taste the dew or chew a blade of grass; feel the ground beneath you. This is what it is to be alive.

Stage 3: Revisiting the Past

When you are rested from your experience, take a look over the notes you made during your time away from the world. In particular, place them alongside the notes you made earlier when you did the conception journey in chapter 3. Do you notice any similarities between the two?

Our experiences in the womb sometimes set us up to hear the messages of fatigue in a particular way. In one burial workshop, Ivy could not wait to get out of her grave. She was twitchy and restless all night. She also, incidentally, was born prematurely and remembered feeling claustrophobic and trapped in the womb because she wanted to get away from her mother (a pattern that had stayed with her for life). Elizabeth, in the grave right next to her, loved being buried and cried when she had to get out. She had been a late arrival as a baby and had enjoyed every moment in her mother's womb.

The messages of fatigue were very different for each of these women as well. Ivy tended to get depressed at life whenever she felt trapped by circumstances or events and was inclined to move on in her relationships with lightning speed, dropping friends and lovers on a frequent basis (and then complaining that she had no friends or lovers!). Whereas Elizabeth found it difficult to move on at all and had been in the same relationship for twelve years, even though it had, as she subtly put it, its "ups and downs."

Knowing how you react to fatigue is one of your defenses against it. As you make it conscious and recognize the pattern in yourself, you can then move on to find balance. Comparing your own "burial" experience with your womb experience may bring you greater clarity around this and help you re-establish balance.

Kami-Dama: A Shrine to Balance

The *kami-dama*, or shelf of the gods, is a *saidan*—a shrine or altar—that has a place in the Shinto homes of Japan and in all Ninja dojo. It is a means of contacting the *kami*—the gods—and drawing their elemental energies into our daily lives through focus on the shrine and the harmonization of our spiritual powers with the flow of the universe.

Just as we find ourselves in the north of the spiral (see the map on page 20) when we are dealing with matters of fatigue and warriorship, so should the kami-dama be placed against the north wall of the home or dojo. The north is regarded as heaven's path—the path to spirit—since the north star is always heaven's first gift to the night.

On each side of the shrine is placed a growing plant or cuttings from the evergreen sakaki tree. The plants represent life and growth, that which endures (is always green), and is therefore unavailable to fatigue.

Three containers are placed on the kami-dama. One holds salt, one rice, and one water: everything that is needed to sustain life. Nine candles are arranged at the front, symbolizing the light we bring to the world and our illumination of the shadows within ourselves.

All of the elements of the Godai are therefore present on the altar. The Fire of the candles, the Water in the container, Air represented by the plants, since plants grow skyward toward the light, and Earth, symbolized by the rice (a gift of the fields) and salt (a gift of the mountains). The kami-dama itself becomes the Void, the interplay between human and god and the creative potential that is held by this threshold place.

Above the shrine are hung pieces of rice paper, cut and folded to look like lightning bolts, symbols of spirit and transformation; and at the center of the dama is placed a mirror, the divine face of truth. Whenever we sit before the dama and look into this mirror, we are in the presence of the gods and reminded of our own divinity. Gods do not fall prey to fatigue because gods are the flow of the universe, in balance, in harmony, at peace with all there is, and this is within us, too. Simple meditation on the Tao and on oneself for a few minutes a day will therefore bring refreshment and the possibility of enlightenment as to the nature of our true selves.

The kami-dama can also be used in a more active way, however, to draw in the qualities we want and to release those things that are not serving us but, through our attachments to them, keep leading us into battles with fatigue. Such an approach is known to the Andean warrior traditions as well, where this shrine to the gods is called the *mesa nortena*, the "northern table."

The Northern Table

Just as the kami-dama is a shrine and not a shelf, the mesa is an altar rather than a table. On it are arranged *artes* (natural and common objects, such as shells, rocks, flowers, swords, torches, statues, dolls, etc.), all of which have a sacred or symbolic content. The way these objects are arranged is significant, as they represent the forces of nature and the cosmos. When a *maestro* (master) of the mesa moves any of these items, he influences nature itself. The mesa has three areas to it: the *campo ganadero* (field of the dark) on the left, the *campo justicero* (field of justice, or field of light) on the right, and the *campo medio* (middle or neutral field), which is the place of balance at the center. By working with these forces and moving the artes between fields, the maestro assists his client to identify the things that are causing disharmony or fatigue in her life and to re-establish balance and order.

This is regarded as spiritual work. But there is a psychological or strategic aspect to it as well, which is that it gives the client an action plan for the future, enabling her to conserve her energies against fatigue by focusing on those things she really needs to do to achieve her goals, and avoid the things that distract her.

Let's say the client has recently lost her job, for example. On the left of the altar, the maestro places artes that symbolically represent the job that was lost. These might be things with both "good" and "bad" associations for the client, because no job is ever perfect. During the process of choosing and placing these artes, the client thus gains perspective on the situation and sees what the job really meant to her, with all of its positives and negatives. She therefore begins to achieve a sense of balance about what she has actually lost, instead of giving away her energies to the suffering or shame that job loss might hold for her. On the right of the altar are placed artes that represent the ideal job the client is now looking for.

The middle section, or neutral field, is where the real work is done, however, because in this area the maestro places items that symbolize the steps that must be taken to get from left to right. The client is therefore clearer on what needs to be done and has an action plan she can follow to let go of the old job and find a new one that is better.

The keys to healing are balance and realism, the very aims of those of us who are seeking to integrate and master the energy of the Soul Warrior. The altar becomes a tool of focus and a means of avoiding fatigue; by using it actively in this way, we can now see clearly where we have come from, where we are going, and how to get there, without losing energy or being distracted on the way.

EXERCISE 22
Creating an Active Kami-Dama

You can create such an altar for any situation where you feel you are lacking balance or losing energy. Or you can create a composite altar, which draws together a number of different elements that all have a bearing on your life.

Remain fully aware throughout the process, so you are not just randomly selecting items (artes) to include, but thinking about each one and what it means for you. The ritual of building the left and right fields should take no less than an hour by the time you have assembled and placed your artes. The neutral field at the center will probably take longer, as this is the place of strategy and balance, where your action plan will form, and it is therefore important to get it right.

Stage 1: Reflection

Begin by assembling the items you will use. This will require a time of meditation or reflection on where you are in your life, where you want to go, the issues that confront you, and the root cause of your fatigue. Don't stint on this; it is one of the most important parts of the process and will help you focus.

Artes can be anything with meaning or symbolic content for you. I have seen car headlamps used on these altars, representing a need in the person's life for illumination or a "path of light through the darkness," kitchen knives to symbolize the need to cut through a particular barrier, and herbs to suggest healing. Whatever you want to include is fine. Don't limit yourself.

Stage 2: Building the Light and Dark Fields

When you have all the items together, pause for a moment and look at them. As a representation of your life, what do these things say about you? What insights do they offer?

Then start to arrange these items, beginning with the dark field (where you have come from) on the left, in a way that makes sense to you. This, too, is a process of insight, because every position has its own symbolic meaning. What does it mean, for example, that you are drawn to place a photograph of an ex-lover next to a cactus or a stone, while a letter from someone else is placed next to a candle? Write down your realizations as they come.

Now build the field of light (where you want to go) on the right-hand side in exactly the same way. The light field represents things that you want to draw into your life, and these can be as idealized or ambitious as you wish. Even if you believe you could never obtain or achieve these things, you should still include them because, at an unconscious level, they still drive you; and it is healthier and less fatiguing to bring them into the light so you can see where your energies are going.

Then too, once you look at these things you have previously dismissed as "impossible," you may realize that they are not so unattainable after all. "If you believe you can or believe you can't, you're right," as Henry Ford once said.

As you build the space, write down your realizations.

Stage 3: Creating Balance

The field on the left is where you are or have been (A); the field on the right is where you want to go (C). To get from A to C there has to be a B. Making this bridge is the job of the neutral field. We most often feel the drain of fatigue when we are unfocused and spreading our energies too thinly. The purpose of the neutral field is to return us to balance by giving us a strategy that contains our energy.

To return to our earlier example, let's say you are dispirited because you have lost your job, and this has had a negative effect on your income. In the dark field you might place a few small coins to symbolize your lack of money, while in the light field you place $10 bills or £20 notes to represent the abundance you want. There are many ways of making money, of course. They range from setting up your own consulting firm, to retraining, to robbing a bank. In warrior terms, every one of these is legitimate as long as you realize its consequences and are prepared to accept responsibility for them. If you are confused or caught between options, however, you will never get the money you want, because you will be chasing every opportunity that presents itself. You will be spreading yourself too thinly and won't be in control of your life.

In this middle section you therefore place artes symbolizing the direction you have chosen as the way you will attract money. These could include a college prospectus if you choose to retrain, or the floor plans of the local bank if you have decided on a different course of action. Whichever you choose is a visible commitment and a means of channeling energy as an act of attention and focus.

As each of your ambitions is fulfilled, make any changes you wish to these fields. In this way, your "shelf of the gods" becomes a work in progress, and you have continued balance and direction in life.

A Strategy for Living

I used the word *strategy* a few times in connection with the dama. To the Ninja, strategy—*heiho*—is a warrior skill. It is a way of avoiding fatigue by honing your intention and giving you a definite objective for your actions in the world.

You have probably heard the expression, *energy flows where attention goes*. This is strategy too. It is holding a thought of how your life will be—with the addition of focus (clarity)—and then releasing this vision to the universe, while living as if your vision were, in a sense, already true. The Ninja know that when we do so the universe sees our commitment and understands we are serious, so it will go out of its way to ensure that we get what we want.

Strategy works with the Tao. You know what you want and hold that in mind as a direction finder for your life; then, your focus is on the things that make it possible. This is not done in a clingy, rigid way. You don't allow your focus to limit you so much that you develop tunnel vision and miss other opportunities that fit your overall plan. Rather, the thought is held as a reminder to yourself. Because you are focused on what you want, your energies automatically follow your intentions.

When we believe and trust that things will go our way, rather than forcing the square things of our lives into the round holes of our needs, we find that, strangely enough, things do start to happen *for us* rather than *to us*—maybe not in the way we thought they would, but in the way they *always* would if only we let them.

Sandra Ingerman, who has recently been conducting remarkable work in transforming environmental toxins and polluted water into clear, drinkable water using only the power of focus and intent, has this to say about strategy: "The power of our imagination can be used by all of us to create a positive present and future. . . . It takes intention, focus and concentration to not get caught up in and distracted by the drama around us and to keep focusing our vision. The key is to see, feel, hear, smell, and taste the life you want to have and the world you want to live in as if it is happening now."*

It *is* happening now. In fact, in some alternate reality just outside the periphery of your vision, it has *already* happened. If you decide to live as if the life you want is already yours, you will make it real.

Controlling Your Folly

My acts are sincere but they are only the acts of an actor because everything I do is controlled folly . . . nothing matters.

—DON JUAN

A warrior makes decisions and sticks to them. The only thing that can change him from his course is a second strategic decision informed by the outcome of the first, not the vicissitudes of fate or a change of heart. And yet a warrior still takes himself lightly and remains relaxed about

---

*You can read more about Sandra's work on the transmutation of matter in her book, *Medicine for the Earth: How to Transform Personal and Environmental Toxins* (New York: Three Rivers Press, 2001).

life, because as well as strategy and focus he is aware of something else—his folly.

A *folly,* in Victorian England, was a ruin deliberately built on the grounds of a house to add interest or spice to its surroundings. (Examples were the faux rubble of a fantasy castle or an old monastery.) We create follies in our lives in the same way, making illusions out of idiosyncrasies and then living them, so that our worlds look grand and interesting. There is nothing wrong with this, as long as we don't start believing our own "press releases" and imagine that we really have a castle and not just a pile of stones.

A folly is something pretend. We pretend we are important, for example, and, through the power of our intention, it may well be that we do become important in financial or social terms. But this success is still illusion, since the social role we play is not who we really are (or all that we are), and our self-importance is only ever transient in the scheme of things. We still have our appointment with death. If we start to believe our image, though, we must give up our energy to the maintenance of folly. Then we inevitably get into scrapes and battles with life to prove to ourselves that we really are this person we believe ourselves to be. At this point, we invite fatigue. Self-importance is always self-defeating in this way.

We can live a folly of the future, allowing unfocused dreams to build fantasy castles for us as if they really mattered, or a folly of the past, where we allow our unreal memories of an unreal life to dictate who we are today. Either way, we are not present with what is, so we are still caught up in illusion.

Because we are alive and we have to believe in something, we will inevitably be living a folly of some kind. The difference for the Soul Warrior is that he understands this and makes a conscious choice to take action anyway. In this, he controls his folly; it does not control him, and he can follow his own path of truth.

So keep it light. Follow your vision and use strategy to make it real, but understand that it's all meaningless anyway. It is freedom and happiness that matter, not giving your energy to sustain an illusion.

Above all, relax. Life is to be played with, not stressed over.

eleven

The Initiation of the Soul Warrior: Staying Awake

Techniques for Overcoming Soul Fatigue

When one is happy there is no time to be fatigued; being happy engrosses the whole attention.

—E. F. Benson

There are degrees of fatigue; and the mood itself, even though it may feel intense at the time, is fleeting for the warrior who can recognize it and let it go as an arising of the mind rather than the onset of a permanent and debilitating state. The warrior sees the bigger picture and has a strategy to keep her on course.

But she may also, from time to time, need a boost of energy for the journey onward when fatigue arises in her. The north of the spiral, the direction of the Soul Warrior, is represented by the Godai element of Earth (chi), and it is here that we find one of our most powerful allies for retaining balance and gathering new strength.

This chapter therefore begins with two techniques for receiving energy from the Earth, for those moments when we need help to get us through or keep us on track toward our vision.

The Earth in Your Blood

For the Ninja, the Earth—chi—represents the most basic need of all warriors for a strong core around which the drifting confusions of life can spin but never penetrate their balance or awareness of a deeper connection to the world.

The Earth is the Ninja's first and most passionate love. It is what sustains him and gives him nourishment. It has always been there as the single constant in his life, and as long as he can touch the Earth, he can draw sustenance from it. The following exercise is a moving meditation to help you draw this energy to yourself.

EXERCISE 23
Reconnection

Take off your shoes, go outside, and connect with the Earth through your feet. Closing your eyes and breathing into your belly, imagine roots growing from your feet and fingers, pushing down into the Earth through all the strata of history—the grass, the soil, the ages of humankind, the old bones of ancestors, the deep mysteries of a planet that has lived for millennia and hosted wonders. Allow these roots to continue growing, and visualize them as they burrow down through years and miles of rock until they reach the molten heart of the Earth's core.

We humans have two suns—one above us in the sky and one at the center of our world. This Earth that we consider "mother" could not exist without the power of "father sun" at its heart. In fact, the Earth is not "feminine" as we conceive it, but a place of balance where male and female energies meet. It is not just our mother, but our father too.* Feel the warmth and power of this second sun, and the heat in your body as you draw its energy up through your roots.

---

*In fact, it is more accurate to say that the Earth is not "male," "female," or any combination of the two. This is a mythos—the projection of human-centric archetypes onto the planet. At its most fundamental level, the Earth is, of course, just a rock spinning in

Now raise your arms and draw down power from the sun above you, so you are caught in the flow of two immense fields of energy, with you as the point of collection, connection, and transformation. Decide how you will use this energy, and employ it with strategy to achieve what you will.

EXERCISE 24
Earth Stone Meditation

For a gentle way of dealing with the experiences of everyday stress, madness, and mayhem, find yourself eight or more flat, round-edged stones, an inch or so in diameter, preferably white. Lie down on your back and place one of these over each chakra point and simply relax for fifteen minutes or so.

Visualize these stones taking away your tension, and see your stresses leave you. The grounding energy of the stones will enter your body, helping to restore and balance your ki.

If you need to work on a particular energy center to help with a current issue in your life, place one stone at the appropriate chakra and hold another two, one in each hand. Spend fifteen minutes in relaxed awareness of energy flowing to the place where it is most needed, and feel your body recharging itself. This works for physical as well as spiritual, mental, or emotional problems.

You know your own body better than anyone else, but as a starting point, you can use the following guide to place the third stone according to the problem you feel you are up against. Besides more obvious physical problems, blockages at chakra points can suggest the following:

---

space and everything else that we "know" about it or believe it to be is a description that we apply. Reducing things to their fundamentals in this way and then deciding what meanings we will *choose*, individually, to give them is also part of the warrior's skills and strategies of clarity.

Soles of the feet: Difficulties in being grounded or fully present

Genitals: Problems with sexuality or insecurity

Solar plexus: Feeling held back or not achieving the things you know you're capable of

Heart: Emotional issues and difficulty connecting with others

Throat: Concerns about speaking your truth or saying what needs to be said

Brow: An inability to focus or see things clearly

Crown of the head: Lack of connection to spirit or confusion about your real purpose in life.

When you are finished, wash the stones in cold salt water and leave them to dry in the sun, after which you can use them again.

Losing Soul

Sometimes, it is not everyday madness we are up against, but something deeper, an energetic pattern in our lives that has led to what some traditions call soul loss. For the Ninja this has associations with the word *kinonai*—"dispirited"—where we have lost some of the vital energy that makes us who we are.

When we are at one with the Tao, it is impossible for our energy to leak away because we are investing ourselves naturally—and only—in what the Shinto religion refers to as "right practice, right sensibility, right attitude." We are just being ourselves, in other words.

In this natural state all manner of miracles may be possible. There are stories, for example, that during World War II, when the Nazis captured and tortured Jack Schwartz (a member of the Dutch resistance), they watched in amazement as the wounds they had inflicted on him healed in seconds before their eyes. When they asked how he did it, Schwartz replied that he was at one with God and the universe (a place the Ninja knew as Void). Of course you can heal yourself if you are one with God; if you're God, you can do anything.

In the same way, Saint Ammachi sucked disease from the wounds of lepers in order to cure them, never once getting sick herself. Asked how this was possible, she replied that anything is possible. When she performed her healings she *was* God—and gods heal others, they do not get ill themselves.*

When we are out of balance, however, the reverse is true, and we can become prone to all manner of physical, emotional, mental, or spiritual disturbances, leading to weakness, fatigue, and depression.

Shinto texts discuss the High Plain of Heaven—a place where we are spiritually in tune—and the Dark Land, an unclean place populated by lost souls and the wandering dead. This land of the dead is the place to which we lose our soul energy through shock or trauma, when our fatigue has simply become too great for us to bear.

The soul part, in its pain, takes flight to this other world and must be guided back to us so we are reunited with these missing fragments of our self and can once again see our true situation and our sacred place in nature.

Soul Healing

The Ninja understanding is that—as we saw in our discussion of Magus energy—it is often the tricks of the mind that prevent us from realizing that we *already* live in a world that is sacred, that holds our truth and will meet our needs if we let it.

"We could say that, at the level of the mind [there is an illusion] that we must come up with a solution to a problem—or [a] feeling that there is a solution or a problem at all. . . . The instruction is to stop. Do something unfamiliar. Do anything besides rushing off in the same old direction, up to the same old tricks."[1]

The advice of the warrior, in other words, is to *not conspire* with the mind that tells us we have lost something and if only it was returned to us all would be well. (This would be giving away our power by agreeing

---

*For more information on these and other "miracles," see Sandra Ingerman's book, *Medicine for the Earth*.

that it has actually been lost and might never return.) Instead, do something about it—"something unfamiliar"—to bring ourselves back into balance.

The philosopher Jean-Paul Sartre remarked, bluntly, that there are two ways to the gas chamber: free or not free. In any set of circumstances—no matter how dire—we can always choose our attitude toward it. For the Ninja, what we have *is* our life, and the way of the warrior is to live it fully.

If the Tao is whispering to you that you must take on your fatigue by healing your soul, then you have every right to do so, and there is a practice to help with this.

In many traditional systems of healing, such as those employed by the mountain Ninja, it is believed that illness and fatigue of the soul, no matter what personal or specific form it takes, arises because primal relationships with Earth have been broken. Healing comes from reconnecting with the natural world.

Healers in Japan still prescribe forest walks and meditative contact with trees (regarded as portals for spirit) as cures for depression, which is believed to arise through soul loss. In Japan, there are many sacred trees, rocks, waterfalls, and other natural shrines and power places to which people bring offerings of sake (rice wine), rice cakes, or flowers so they may spend time in the healing presence of nature.

Soul Cleansing Breath

Sometimes there is a breathing exercise that accompanies this nature meditation. One of these was developed by Mikao Usui (1865–1926), founder of what we now know as *Usui Reiki Ryoho* (the Method of Personal Perfection), one of the first systems of reiki (a word which, in Japanese, means "happiness"). The breathwork used in this method is called *joshin kokyu ho* (soul cleansing breath).

The approach is to focus on the *tandien* (a place in the body located about two inches below the navel), placing your hands on your lap with your palms facing upward and then breathing slowly in through the nose.

As you breathe in, visualize a white healing light carried in on your breath and expanding to fill your body. This white light is a purifier and will cleanse you of negativity, while restoring your soul as you draw in the healing powers of nature.

As you breathe out, visualize this light drifting out of your body, through your skin, into infinity in all directions, carrying with it your cares and returning them to nature, where this energy is transformed and becomes the breath of the Tao.

At the beginning and end of each breath, Usui encouraged his students to pause for a moment and reflect on the five simple truths. These five truths he had come to understand, through a lifetime of study, as the working of the Tao which, if practiced wholeheartedly, would fend off disease so that soul loss and fatigue do not become issues for us at all. The beauty of these truths is that we are asked to put them into practice "just for today"; there is no pressure upon us to be saints throughout our lives, but just to act in the immediate term—to be here now.

Just for today, in that moment between in-breath and out-breath . . .
Forget about anger
Forget about worry
Be grateful
Do your spiritual work
Be kind to others (and yourself)

EXERCISE 25
Restoring Your Soul

Take yourself to a place in nature where you feel connected to the Earth and which is still and has a sense of calm about it, then sit down, close your eyes, and relax. Begin your soul cleansing breath.

Whatever energy blockage is between you and the Tao, representing itself as fatigue or a loss of soul, it has a form in the world. It could be the breakup of a relationship, an illness, or the loss of a job, but somewhere in the flow of things it began as energy before it became a physical presence. What is the thing that has gone wrong for you?

Whatever it is, hold it in mind and let an image form of its energetic counterpart, the essence it had before it became a physical or material concern. See this as the Spirit of Fatigue, not an enemy here to hurt you, but an honest friend who can give you advice on your life. Talk to this being.

What is the message from Fatigue? What can you learn from it? What can you do to change things for the future and reassure this spirit that its message has been heard and it is free now to go? Ask as many questions as you need to, then thank this Spirit of Fatigue for its advice.

Before you say goodbye to this spirit, however, ask for a symbol of some kind, one that represents the possibility of a better future. As you continue your soul cleansing breath, draw in the energy of this symbol and let it charge your own spirit as, with the out-breath, you release to the universe the fatigue that you feel in your soul. When you feel yourself lighter and more energized, breathe out and open your eyes.

Make your offering to this place in nature that has helped you let go of pain (flowers or a little rice or tobacco is fine) and then return home. Whatever the symbol that was offered to you by the Spirit of Fatigue, take paints, pens, crayons, modeling clay, or whatever you wish, and create it as an anchor for your more empowered soul.

Shizen No Kamae: Earth Movement

The Ninja fighting posture that reflects the stability of the Earth is *shizen no kamae*. It is also called the *natural posture*, because it looks and feels as if you are just standing as you might naturally do at any time. The American Ninja, Stephen Hayes, was surprised at the simplicity of this posture too, until his teacher, Tanemura, reminded him: "Of course. If a man [or woman, or situation] is intent on harming or killing you, he is not likely to inform you first. You must begin to protect yourself from the second you perceive his intentions. You will usually be standing or walking in such a pose as this."[2]

It is the same with life. The things that cause us fatigue will often come out of nowhere, and all at once, just when everything seemed to be going okay. They may be tiny and inconsequential in themselves but cumulatively they can add up to a massive assault and suddenly mean so much more, becoming a pattern of significance that ties into our whole life story.

Practicing this moving meditation can help you maintain a degree of relaxed preparedness for these left hooks from life by getting your body in action and quickening your mind.

Moving meditation may seem something of a misnomer, in fact, because your intention with this posture is actually to *not* move (to not move away, at least) but simply to remain out of reach of fatigue without having to expend too much energy or resort to drastic action. You stay centered, solid, confident, and grounded in all that you do; you are just unavailable to be harmed.

Begin with your legs hip-width apart, knees straight but soft, so you are not straining, and your spine (in fact, your whole body) relaxed. Your arms hang at your sides, palms inward, as if you were standing naturally in conversation.

Now imagine that an opponent (life) takes a swing at you. Simply duck beneath it, keeping your back straight, so the blow sails harmlessly past you. As you touch the Earth, palms down, scoop up the ki (life force) that emanates from it and, as you slowly stand up straight again, raise your arms out and to the side, then to the top of your head with your palms facing down toward your body. Feel the energy of the Earth cascade over you and let it fill you with serenity and power.

Earth Breathing

The Earth is solid, immutable, undefeatable, which is the feeling you want when you sense yourself under attack or are faced with the uncertainty, tiredness, or spiritual depression that can lead to fatigue. This breathing meditation allows these qualities of the Earth to become part of your energy and to fortify you.

Stand or sit comfortably and, filling your lungs slowly, visualize the air you take in as a heavy force that sinks to the bottom of your belly. Allow your stomach to expand fully as you breathe in. As the air fills you, it radiates peace, calm, and certainty into your middle, holding you fast to the Earth through its own weight, and then diffuses outward to cover your entire body.

Repeat this meditation before any encounter where you might have problems, or whenever you want stillness of mind and spirit.

WARRIOR COMMITMENT

I Relax into Freedom and Become the Soul Warrior

I am as solid as the Earth and unavailable to any conflict that might swerve me from my vision of how *I* want to live.

I commit to trust so I can relax into life and allow the Tao to do its work unhindered by my worries or concerns. I am in tune with what is, and I allow my life to flourish.

I am faithful to my truth and I make this commitment to myself in full consciousness, to honor myself, and in recognition of my right to be here as a part of this Earth which would be so much less without me.

I let this commitment go to the universe, while allowing its energy to guide and support me, and I believe and trust that things will be this way.

SIGNED:_____

DATE:_____

making Life your artform

Art is never decoration, embellishment; instead, it is work of enlightenment. Art, in other words, is a technique for acquiring liberty . . . developed by reflection within the soul.

—BRUCE LEE

The Grotte de Lombrives in the Ariege region of France is one of the largest cave systems in the world. Deep underground there are petrified waterfalls, stalagmites as big as cars, and a vast main chamber three times the size of Notre Dame Cathedral.

It was in these caves that the Cathars sought sanctuary from the Inquisition and the Resistance hid from the Nazis, and they have been home to many other rebels, revolutionaries, warriors, and freedom-fighters throughout history.

The cave walls are, in places, covered with pictures, poetry, and graffiti, some of it dating back a thousand years; art that tells the story of hundreds of lives and centuries of free-thinking; a reminder that real progress only comes from those who stand outside the norm and see a better world.

Revolution is the secret of the Void. Commit to your every day as if the life you are making is itself a form of art. Scrawl your name and paint yourself all over it. Then you join the immortals.

Art is coming face to face with yourself.

—JACKSON POLLOCK

twelve

ku (voiD): SpiRAliNG iNTO The voiD

Through the Gates for the First Time—
Becoming the Mystic and Elder

Art . . . never finished, only abandoned.

—LEONARDO DA VINCI

The final initiatory test for the con-
temporary Ninja in every training dojo is to face his death, calmly, present in the moment, and through that gesture, to touch the Void and
make a visible affirmation that he will live his life according to his own
intent.

The student kneels before the sensei, his back toward his teacher,
eyes closed, focused on his breath. Behind him, his teacher holds a sword
with a "live" blade, sharp and lethal. At any moment, without warning,
the sensei will bring this blade quickly down to the center of his student's
head.

The work of the initiate is to sense the moment and, before the blade
lands, to roll out of harm's way, springing back up to face his teacher in
a combat position in case there is a second strike. The teacher, symbolically, murders the student; the student refuses the teacher and commits
to his life, no matter what, even if it means leaving the man who has

been his mentor for many years. In that moment there is freedom for them both, and the master-pupil ties are cut.

If the initiate moves too quickly during this test, he has failed; if he moves too slowly or not at all, he is dead. How then does he know the precise moment in which to dive away?

The student is instructed throughout his training to let go, relax, to center himself and become one with the Void. During this final test, it is assumed that he has learned these lessons and dealt with his issues of fear, powerlessness, lack of clarity, and soul fatigue, and can therefore blend with the all-that-is. He should be so at one with the creative impulse of the universe that there is no separation between him and his teacher.

It is not that he gauges or guesses the moment of the strike; he *becomes* the strike because he is his teacher's thoughts. It is not that he hears the split-second whisper of the blade through air; he *is* the blade, he *is* the air. Dodging the cut is therefore simplicity itself: he just moves, not through time or space because those concepts have long disappeared, but from one thought to another. This is what carries him to safety: He simply wills it so.

The Void is the ultimate destination, if not the primary goal of a warrior. All warriors begin their quest looking only for freedom and happiness. They may find, however, that something remarkable happens as they make their journey through the Four Gates: not only do they learn mastery of themselves, they begin to see beneath the surface of reality and find a connection to something bigger than themselves.

Ninja know this "something bigger" as ku—the Void. It is the place of One-Self (oneself) and of no-self, where we are once again a part of all things, exactly as we were when we were first born.

The initiate who has mastered the energies of courage, power, clarity, and spirit, and who stands as a Soul Warrior, will naturally come to this place in time. All he has to do is remember his lessons and hold fast to his truth and he will find (or be found by) it, for the natural fate or reward of the Soul Warrior is to evolve into the Mystic who can look at the world with wisdom and compassion, laughter and silence, knowing that so-called reality (the societal life we live) is only one tiny part of the infinite mind.

In tribal societies like those of the Ninja, the job of the Mystic is to become the Elder—the *Jonin* (leader) or *Binwanka* (man of ability)—the role model and guide for those who seek initiation and wish to make the journey of the Four Gates for themselves. It is the desire and the purpose of the Elder to serve.

Our failure to initiate our young in Western society is one of the overriding problems of our age.* Now that you have been through your initiation, I hope you will be inspired to teach what you know, as you mature into Mystic and Elder. This means right action and right thinking in the world—setting a good example—not just the formal instructing of another, or handing this book to them.

Becoming the Mystic means turning your life into living art, as it is your behavior and how you hold yourself that creates a world worth passing on. There is a duty of care when you become the Mystic, because every life you touch will change the world in some way.

Robert Byrne wrote humorously that "There are two kinds of people: those who finish what they start—and so on." Accepting your responsibilities with courage and for the good of all makes you one of the rarest of people on Earth: someone who finishes what they started.

Touching the Void

The Void is not just a different level of understanding; it is a different *quality* of understanding. It is the awareness of a new world that we are also always a part of, where "what is seen is transient, what is unseen is eternal,"[1] and the knowledge—somehow, and without words—that the

---

*A recent television documentary revealed that suicide is now the biggest killer for men in the United Kingdom who are in their twenties. Our young men have more chance, statistically, of dying by their own hand than in a car accident. If nothing else, this shows a lack of meaning in their lives or reason to continue living. It is the job of the Elder to provide that reason, so this tragedy does not continue. (*Picking Up the Pieces* was televised in the United Kingdom on Channel 4, August 2, 2004.)

essence of this world is love with no separation or conditions attached.

The Mystic, having made the spiral journey, returns, in a sense, to who he was: the Lover. Except now his community is not just himself and those closest to him, but the entire world that he offers himself in service to.

We who are still on the journey can't know much of the Void because we have not yet reached it. Sometimes we may catch a glimpse. But the paradox is that we can't know much of it when we get to the end of our journey either, since we then become part of the Void, one with it, and inseparable from it. The Void flows through us and just is; the Mystic makes no separation between himself and it.

We can get the merest sense of the Void though, before we mature into the Mystic and experience it for ourselves, if we remain open to the fact that everything in the world is energy, and we are that too. We are the breath of the universe, and as co-creators of that universe, we give form to the world.

EXERCISE 26
You Are All There Is

Close your eyes for a moment and ask yourself, *Where do I end and the rest of the world begin?* At a microscopic level, our atoms blend with the air and the earth around us, and whenever we touch a tree or the sky or a lover, our atoms—our bodies—become part of theirs. We are all things.

Imagine what it is to be part of the infinite: energy pulsing from you to merge with the stars. You may become the laughter of children, the birth pains of galaxies, your breath the warmth in the smile of a lover, the heat of a late summer's day, your heartbeat the light from the sun. All of these things are your brothers and sisters, the exact same energy as you. As you spiral into the Void, you are aware of life everywhere, and all of it is you, as you are it. There never were any fears, power games, confusions, fatigues, no gateways to step through, because there never was any separation. There is nothing to fight, nothing to resist, no challenges to face.

"The Ninja looks at the universe as a single, ever-moving process, rather than countless isolated objects or actions. . . . Once we realize that we are working parts of the process, we free ourselves from the notion that we are mere victims in life, taunted by gods and devils. . . . It is these advanced levels of power that are said to give the Ninja 'the mind and eyes of God.'"[2]

Open your eyes and look around you. And know that everything is just as it should be, and just as it ever was.

Becoming Your Primal Self

Return to the primal source where truth has it roots. Repose in the nothing.

—Bruce Lee

The real job of the Mystic is to do nothing more and be nothing more than she already is. The Mystic has experienced the world and learned from the journey. She is confident in herself and aware of her abilities. She *knows* because she has *experienced* her truth, not absorbed it from books or been told it by someone else—and she also knows she does not need to prove anything to herself or to anyone else.

No matter how young or how old such a person is, she is both Elder and newborn, a walker between worlds, connected to the infinite and rooted to the Earth; the great transformer who carries sacred wisdom back to her people and planet. The Mystic is the wild man or woman, the epitome of our primal self, unfettered by social commands, who can cut to the heart of truth beyond the dogma and rhetoric.

Free of ego, this primal self does not have the same desperate hunger to lead or to be right as our sometimes self-appointed moral, religious, or political experts; and the Mystic is therefore the best leader of all, because his judgment can be trusted and his integrity is sound. It is precisely because he does not need to be heard that we should listen carefully to what he says.

The Mystic has no personal agenda but his interest in life. His controlled folly is to foster freedom and self-exploration uncluttered by old paradigms of accepted and "self-evident" truths. He does not teach, he invites learning. He does not preach, he invites discussion. He does not dictate, he invites self-discovery. It is not what he *does* but also *what he does not do,* how he models his integrity and inspiration to others, that makes him wise.

It is hard and it can be lonely if you decide to become a guide and mentor in this way, because we have all grown up without real leaders, no Mystics or Elders to show us the way, and because society itself is defended against new and creative inspirations which might threaten its status quo. But we must start somewhere if the chain is to be broken. And it will get easier with time, as more pioneers of the spirit and more initiated men and women join the rank of Elder beside you.

As Arthur Schopenhauer said: "All truth passes through three stages. First, it is ridiculed. Second, it is violently opposed. Third, it is accepted as being self-evident."

Inner Knowing

The most important thing for a warrior is to trust his inner knowing— the voice of the primal self that connects him to the Void and the essence of the universe. If you allow it to, this inner knowing will speak to you from beyond the socialized self and offer you a truth and clarity you can depend upon when life throws new questions and doubts your way.

EXERCISE 27
Hearing the Primal Self

Stand up, close your eyes, and relax. Take your attention to your genitals, which is where the primal urge for life is located. Imagine you have a circle of energy within you, which travels from your genitals, up through your belly, your solar plexus (the place of will), your heart (the place of compassion), your throat (where personal truth is spoken), through your head, down your back, and closes the loop as it reaches your genitals again. Let this energy flow for a few minutes and feel how it is to connect with the power of this primal fire. Then gather all of this energy together and, in one burst, send it out from your belly as it rushes up your body.

Project your energy out a few feet in front of you, and there (in whatever form it naturally takes or whatever seems to fit) see the image of your Primal Self standing before you. It may look like an archetypal wise man, a magical crone, a Tibetan sage, an Assyrian priestess, an animal, or even some pre- or superhuman form. It really doesn't matter how it looks; it is only important for you to know that this entity has access to all the wisdom of the Void.

Ask whatever questions you want, or simply make a contract between you that from now on you will listen to what your Primal Self has to say and he or she will communicate with you in a way that makes the message crystal clear. Do not be afraid to ask for proof, so you will know that you can trust this advice in future. Ask for information you can act on now, something simple and easy to perform but which gives you the sense of validation you need that you are right to do what your inner wisdom is guiding you to. Open your eyes when you are ready and, whatever you have been advised to do, act on it.

The Ninja say that we should allow ourselves nine days to notice the effects our actions create. Look for omens, synchronicities, symbols, coincidences, dreams—anything "nonrational"—during this time. This is your proof, and once you have it, you will know you can trust yourself to make the right decisions intuitively.

Ku (Void): The Universal Experience of Freedom

Within the *gorin kuji myo himitsu shaku* (the Ninja system of mysticism), there is a mudra (a hand posture to focus energy) that is used to tune in to the scheme of totality that is the Void. It is known as *kuji-in* and is a way of channeling universal forces with intention and strategy. The Ninja would use this whenever they felt disconnected from the flow of things, out of balance, or subject to doubt about their course of action and place in the world. It is a gesture for serenity and certainty.

EXERCISE 28
The Kuji-In *for the Void*

Starting with your little fingers, interlink them, curling them together at the second knuckle. Do the same with the next two fingers of each hand, but not your index fingers. Bring your index fingers together at the tips instead and, keeping them straight, point them forward and away from you. Your thumbs also meet at the tips and point upward so your index fingers and thumbs make an L shape. Now place your hands against your solar plexus, the seat of your will.

As you do so, see the energy of the Void channeled down through your thumbs, which act as antennae, and moving out ahead of you through your index fingers. Walk forward, following these beams of light that focus your intention.

In any situation of doubt, no matter where you are, you can quietly and inconspicuously bring your hands together in this way and balance your breathing. This will help you overcome whatever difficulties you face.

A Return to First Questions

I said in chapter 4 that I would be surprised if you gained any really useful insight from Exercise 2, when you chose among the unfinished sentences to complete. That isn't strictly true (although it was at the time). Participants in Four Gates workshops often find, in fact, that while the sentence they chose so seemingly at random is only marginally relevant to them at the start of their journey, it reveals itself at the end to be the one central issue they have been wrestling with all along; the very thing, in fact, that is their greatest challenge and greatest separation from the Void.

Go back to this exercise and look again at your own choice of sentence, now that you have taken this journey. You too may find it has much deeper meaning for you now, knowing that everything you do in life is an expression of yourself and that all things are in some way connected. Answering this question again may start you on your journey for a second or even a third time as you deepen into ownership of the Mystic role, because, after all, life goes on, and we change and grow. Perhaps we must all walk this path many times. And each time we do, we find more wisdom and insight to help us perform the job of Elder.

Tomorrow is the most important thing in life.
It's perfect when it arrives and it puts itself in our hands.
It hopes we've learned something from yesterday.

—John Wayne

EXERCISE 29
Finding Your Song

There is a blaze from the center, the heart of all things. Life!
From galaxies to photons. Life! Life is conscious, intelligent
energy. . . . It sings to everyone around it of its existence. This is
life energy being scattered out as a gift from the heart. An indi-
vidual's song is its joy. And we share our songs with each other
continually. This is our web of joy.

—Domano Hetaka

Close your eyes and let your breath fill your body. Now imagine a cord of blue spiral energy emerging from your crown and winding up into the night sky, then attaching itself to a star which, in turn, sends its energy out to the next star, and that one to the next, and so on, until you perceive all of the points of light in the universe linked together in one giant web with you at its center. That is the way life is. Feel how your minute movements cause the entire web to vibrate and set your own body vibrating with this energy too, as if a string is being played, part of the symphony of all things.

The idea that we are all strings within one symphony is not just an archaic spiritual one or simply an analogy of some kind. String theory is also the latest description quantum physicists have to offer us of how the universe actually works—that we are all energetic vibrations or harmonics played as if on a cosmic string.[3]

Let your body move to this vibration if you wish, and capture the sound of its symphony in your mind, allowing your own musical note to form so that you harmonize with the song of the universe. Sing your note out loud, and let it develop to become your personal Song of Being. Without your contribution to this symphony the world would be less rich. We need you—you are vital to the harmony of all that is.

Open your eyes and, if your song has words, write them down so you remember them. Sing your song often, and let others hear your voice.

Blessings

The Bodhisattva is like the mightiest of warriors, but his enemies are not common foes of flesh and bone. His fight is with the inner delusions. . . . He is the real hero, calmly facing any hardship in order to bring peace, happiness, and liberation to the world.

—The Thirteenth Dalai Lama

I wish you all of this—peace, happiness, and liberation. Most of all I wish you love.

WARRIOR COMMITMENT

My Life Is My Art, My Place the Center,
My Home the Void

I make the Void my home. I allow its wisdom to inform me and its energy to infuse me. I continue my walk around this spiral of life, moving closer to the center, with my spirit to guide my journey.

I am perfect in the eyes of the universe, in this and every moment. I give myself permission to fail and I give myself permission to succeed, knowing that success and failure are the same things—not outcomes in themselves but simply reminders of my purpose in being here. I give myself permission to LIVE.

I offer my life as an example to others who are crying out for peace, freedom, and happiness because they have not found initiation for themselves. I commit myself to the role of Mystic, Elder, and guide to them by living well, in happiness and freedom for myself, so I can be their example. I give myself permission to LOVE.

I let this commitment go to the universe, knowing it will support me, and I believe and trust that things will be this way.

SIGNED:_____

DATE:_____

The day will come when, after harnessing space, the winds, the tides and gravitation, we shall harness the energies of Love. And on that day, for the second time in the history of the world, we shall have discovered Fire.

—TEILHARD DE CHARDIN

NOTES

Preface

1. Stephen K. Hayes, *The Ninja and Their Secret Fighting Art* (Rutland, Vt.: Tuttle Publishing, 1992).

Introduction

1. Bruce Lee, *The Tao of Jeet Kune Do* (Burbank, Calif.: Ohara Publications, 1975).
2. Jack Hoban, *Ninpo: Living and Thinking as a Warrior* (London: Contemporary Books, 1988).
3. Ibid.
4. Lee, *The Tao of Jeet Kune Do.*
5. Hoban, *Ninpo: Living and Thinking as a Warrior.*

Chapter One

1. Masaaki Hatsumi, *The Way Of The Ninja: Secret Techniques* (Tokyo: Kodansha International [JPN], 2004).
2. Ian McEwan, *Saturday* (New York: Nan A. Talese [Random House], 2005).
3. Malidoma Somé, *Of Water and the Spirit* (New York: Penguin Books, 1995).
4. Carlos Castaneda, *The Fire From Within* (New York: Washington Square Press, 1991).
5. Robert Moore and Douglas Gillette, *King, Warrior, Magician, Lover: Rediscovering the Archetypes of the Mature Masculine* (San Francisco: HarperSanFrancisco, 1991).
6. Geo Trevarthen, personal communication, 2004.
7. Carlos Castaneda, *The Eagle's Gift* (New York: Pocket Books, 1982).

Chapter Two

1. Carl Gustav Jung, Collected Works of C. G. Jung, Volume 9 (Part 1): *Archetypes and the Collective Unconscious* (Princeton, N.J.: Princeton University Press, 1969).
2. Howard Thurman, in Sam Keen, *Fire in the Belly: On Being a Man* (New York: Bantam, 1992).
3. Ram Dass, *Be Here Now* (Three Rivers, Mich.: Three Rivers Press, 1971).
4. Carlos Castaneda, *The Teachings of Don Juan: A Yaqui Way of Knowledge* (New York: Penguin Arkana, 1990).
5. Hayes, *The Ninja and Their Secret Fighting Art.*

Chapter Three

1. Ross Heaven, *The Journey To You* (New York: Bantam, 2001).
2. Thomas Verny and John Kelly, *The Secret Life of the Unborn Child* (New York: Time Warner, 1993).
3. Ibid.
4. Jeanine and Frederick Baker and Tamara Slayton, *Conscious Conception: Elemental Journey Through the Labyrinth of Sexuality* (Berkeley, Calif.: North Atlantic Books, 1987).
5. Christopher Hansard, *The Tibetan Art of Living* (London: Hodder Mobius, 2002).
6. Castaneda, *The Eagle's Gift.*

Chapter Four

1. C. Smith and B. Lloyd, "Maternal Behavior and Perceived Sex of Infant: Revisited," *Child Development* 49 (1978), 1263–65.
2. Dr. Arthur Janov, *The Primal Scream: Primal Therapy—the Cure for Neurosis* (London: Abacus, 1990).

Chapter Five

1. Christopher Hansard, *The Tibetan Art of Living.*
2. Pema Chodron, *When Things Fall Apart: Heart Advice for Difficult Times* (Boston: Shambhala, 2000).
3. Ram Dass, *Still Here: Embracing Aging, Changing, and Dying* (New York: Riverhead Books, 2000).
4. P. D. Ouspensky, in Colin Wilson, *The Strange Life of P. D. Ouspensky* (London: Aquarian Press, 1993).
5. Pema Chodron, *When Things Fall Apart.*
6. Castaneda, *The Teachings of Don Juan: A Yaqui Way of Knowledge.*
7. Bill Hicks, *Love All the People: Letters, Lyrics, Routines,* John Lahr, ed. (London: Constable & Robinson, 2000).
8. Hayes, *The Ninja and Their Secret Fighting Art.*

Chapter Six

1. Robert Bly, *Iron John: A Book About Men* (New York: Vintage, 1992).
2. See Robin Skynner and John Cleese, *Families and How to Survive Them* (London: Cedar Books, 1993).
3. See my Web site—www.VodouShaman.com—for details on the geis as the basis for GeisWork™ workshops, which include exercises on conscious conception, the prebirth experience, ancestral healing, and defusing the life script.
4. Robert Bly, *Iron John: A Book About Men.*
5. Joseph Campbell, *The Hero With A Thousand Faces,* Bollingen Series XVII (Princeton, N.J.: Princeton University Press, 1973).

Chapter Seven

1. See Ross Heaven, *The Journey To You.*
2. Thich Nhat Hanh, *The Miracle of Mindfulness* (Boston: Beacon Press, 1999).
3. Hayes, *The Ninja and Their Secret Fighting Art.*

Chapter Eight

1. In Viktor Frankl, *Man's Search For Meaning* (London: Rider, 2004). [Originally published in German in 1946, under the title: *Ein Psycholog erlebt das Konzentrationslager.* First published in English in 1959 under the title: *From Death-Camp to Existentialism.*]
2. Ibid.
3. See, for example, Peter Ainsworth, *Psychology, Law, and Eyewitness Testimony* (Hoboken, N.J.: John Wiley & Sons, 1998).
4. Elizabeth F. Loftus, *Memory: Surprising New Insights into How We Remember and Why We Forget* (Upper Saddle River, N.J.: Pearson/Longman Higher Education, 1981).
5. Noam Chomsky, *Understanding Power: The Indispensable Chomsky,* Peter Mitchell and John Shoeffel, eds. (New York: New Press, 2002).
6. Castaneda, *The Teachings of Don Juan: A Yaqui Way of Knowledge.*

Chapter Nine

1. Carlos Castaneda—City Lights lecture, San Francisco, 1980.
2. The full version of this bushido is in *The Awakened Warrior: Living with Courage, Compassion and Discipline,* Rick Fields, ed. (London: Jeremy P. Tarcher/Putnam, 1994).
3. Stephen K. Hayes, *Ninjutsu: The Art of the Invisible Warrior* (London: Contemporary Books, 1984).

Chapter Ten

1. Frankl, *Man's Search For Meaning*.
2. Ibid.
3. Dr. Dina Glouberman, *The Joy of Burnout: How the End of the World Can Be a New Beginning* (Maui, Hawaii: Inner Ocean Publishing, 2003).
4. Daideoji Yeuzan and Thomas Cleary, *The Code of the Samurai: A Contemporary Translation of the Bushido Shoshinshu of Taira Shigesuke* (Rutland, Vt.: Tuttle Publishing, 2000).
5. Miyamoto Musashi, *Book of Five Rings: The Classic Guide to Strategy*, a 17th century manuscript, published in book form (New York: Gramercy, 1988).

Chapter Eleven

1. Pema Chodron, *When Things Fall Apart*.
2. Hayes, *Ninjutsu: The Art of the Invisible Warrior*.

Chapter Twelve

1. St. Paul, Corinthians 4.16–5.4.
2. Hayes, *The Mystic Arts of the Ninja* (New York: McGraw-Hill, 1985).
3. See, for example, Michio Kaku, *Hyperspace: A Scientific Odyssey Through Parallel Universes, Time Warps, and the 10th Dimension* (New York: Anchor, 1995).

workshops, books, tapes, and trips by ross heaven

Ross Heaven is a therapist and workshop leader based in the United Kingdom who runs courses and trainings internationally on the themes and contents of this and his other books, which include *The Journey To You, Spirit In the City, Vodou Shaman,* and *Darkness Visible.* He has also produced *Infinite Journeys,* a tape of trance drumming suitable as an accompaniment to the meditations described in these books. Ross facilitates spiritual journeys to work with healers and visionaries from warrior traditions around the world. Details of all of these products and services are available at www.VodouShaman.com, or via the publisher at the address in the front of this book.

Acknowledgments and Thanks

This book is for my children: my daughters Amelia and Jodie and my son Ocean (because "Once you know your *story,* you can *choose* your truth"). It is also for Arran (for the same reason). And a big hug to Teertha and baby Jaiden.

Thank you to . . .

Damien Rice and Bernadette—for support, permissions, and a night out in Brixton.

Sensei Gary Arthur—for training.

Ram Chatlani, legal genius and spiritual Master—for services to truth and justice.

Simon Buxton—for your never-less-than-valuable insights into what "friendship," "integrity," and "spirit-driven" really mean.

And Saffron, true *Hinin*—for insights into geis and laughs along the Way. May God's love be with you, always (or at least till the end of verse one)!

INDEX

Books of Related Interest

Vodou Shaman
The Haitian Way of Healing and Power
by Ross Heaven

Plant Spirit Shamanism
Traditional Techniques for Healing the Soul
by Ross Heaven and *Howard G. Charing*

Darkness Visible
Awakening Spiritual Light through Darkness Meditation
by Ross Heaven and Simon Buxton

Bone Marrow Nei Kung
Taoist Techniques for Rejuvenating the Blood and Bone
by Mantak Chia

Martial Arts Teaching Tales of Power and Paradox
Freeing the Mind, Focusing Chi, and Mastering the Self
by Pascal Fauliot

Nei Kung
The Secret Teachings of the Warrior Sages
by Kosta Danaos

The Martial Arts of Ancient Greece
Modern Fighting Techniques from the Age of Alexander
by Kostas Dervenis and Nektarios Lykiardopoulos

Iron Shirt Chi Kung
by Mantak Chia

Inner Traditions • Bear & Company
P.O. Box 388
Rochester, VT 05767
1-800-246-8648
www.InnerTraditions.com

Or contact your local bookseller